The Ultimate Pancreatitis Diet Guide

Sadia .L Hardy

All rights reserved. Copyright © 2023 Sadia .L Hardy

COPYRIGHT © 2023 Sadia .L Hardy

All rights reserved.

No part of this book must be reproduced, stored in a retrieval system, or shared by any means, electronic, mechanical, photocopying, recording, or otherwise, without written permission from the publisher.

Every precaution has been taken in the preparation of this book; still the publisher and author assume no responsibility for errors or omissions. Nor do they assume any liability for damages resulting from the use of the information contained herein.

Legal Notice:

This book is copyright protected and is only meant for your individual use. You are not allowed to amend, distribute, sell, use, quote or paraphrase any of its part without the written consent of the author or publisher.

Introduction

This book serves as a comprehensive guide to navigating the dietary landscape when dealing with pancreatitis. Understanding the basics of pancreatitis is crucial, and the cookbook begins by delving into the physiology of the pancreas, the types of pancreatitis, and the causes and symptoms associated with this condition. Readers are then introduced to the 5 Steps of Pancreatitis Diet & Exercises, shedding light on essential lifestyle modifications.

Recognizing the importance of avoiding certain foods, the cookbook provides a detailed list of Foods to Avoid While Having Pancreatitis, emphasizing the significance of making mindful dietary choices. The section on Pancreatitis Attack Prevention Measures offers valuable insights into safeguarding against potential flare-ups.

Lifestyle Recommendations for Pancreatitis Patients extend beyond dietary considerations. Emphasizing the necessity of staying hydrated with "Drink Lots of Water" and incorporating physical activity for weight management, the cookbook offers a holistic approach to managing pancreatitis.

The heart of the Pancreatitis Diet Cookbook lies in its diverse and carefully crafted recipes. Beginning with nourishing "Breakfast Recipes" and moving through the day with "Lunch Recipes," readers are treated to a variety of options that align with pancreatitis dietary guidelines. Basic recipes, savory dishes, meat and fish creations, and comforting soups and stews cater to different tastes and preferences.

Recognizing the importance of snacking, the cookbook introduces "Snack Recipes" that are not only delicious but also pancreatitis-friendly. A dedicated section on "Dessert Recipes" ensures that those with a sweet tooth can indulge without compromising their health. For those looking for refreshing options, "Smoothies Recipes" provides nutritious and enjoyable choices.

Completing the culinary journey, "Staples, Sauces, and Dressings" rounds out the cookbook, offering essential elements to enhance flavor without sacrificing digestive health.

This book stands as a valuable resource, providing not only recipes but also essential information and guidelines to empower individuals in managing their diet and lifestyle while dealing with pancreatitis. With a focus on nourishing and delicious options, this cookbook is a companion on the journey to wellness.

Contents

BASICS OF PANCREATITIS 1
Physiology of the Pancreas 1
Pancreatitis types 2
Causes and Symptoms of Pancreatitis..3
5 Steps of Pancreatitis Diet & Exercises 5
Foods to Avoid While Having Pancreatitis 5
Foods with Pancreatitis to Avoid 5
Pancreatitis Attack Prevention Measures 7
Lifestyle Recommendations for PancreatitisPatients 10
Drink Lots of Water 11
Physical activity to hasten weight loss 12
How the Pancreatitis Diet Differs from OtherDiets 14
BREAKFAST RECIPES 17
Pancakes Wraps 17
Cinnamon Glazed Waffle Rolls 18
Spinach & Quinoa Muffins 19
Overnight Oat Pudding Jar 20
Zucchini & Chickpeas Frittata 21
Oat Pudding with Chia Seeds...22
Quick & Easy Shakshuka 23
Scramble Egg Whites Wrap..23
Asparagus & Tomato Omelet...24
Kale & Quinoa Breakfast Bowl 26
Muesli Breakfast Bowl With Berries 27
Greek Yogurt with Fig Mulberries Pumpkin Seed 27
Sweet Potato Omelet Pie 28
LUNCH RECIPES 30
Hatch Chile "Refried" Beans...31
Indian Butter Chickpeas 32
Mediterranean Quinoa With Pepperoncini 33

Coco-Nutty Brown Rice 34

Herbed Harvest Rice 34

Veggie "Fried" Quinoa 35

Chicken Salad Delight 36

Parsley Burger..37

Seasoned Pork Chops...37

Taco Stuffing...38

Jalapeno Popper Chicken 39

Tuna Au Poivre 40

Fish Stew..41

Grilled Salmon With Fruit And SesameVinaigrette 42

BASIC RECIPES 45

Mixed Greens Salad with Honeyed Dressing 46

Apricot Salad with Mustardy Dressing 47

Potato Caraway with Lemony Fillet 48

Vinegary Berry with Orange Salad 49

Cucumber and Spinach with Chicken Salad...50

Lemony Zucchini with Vinegary Salmon 51

Milky Carrot with Oniony Ginger Soup...51

Garlicky Broccoli with Cashew Soup 52

Squashy Carrot and Celery Soup 53

Mixed Greens Soup with Coconut Milk..54

Onion Chipotle Soup with Sage..55

Pears with Peppered Fennel Soup 56

Scallion with Minty Cucumber Salad 57

SAVORY RECIPES 59

Delicious Buckwheat with Mushrooms & GreenOnions...60

Yummy Chicken and Sweet Potato Stew 61

Healthy Fried Brown Rice with Peas & Prawns 62

Asparagus Quinoa & Steak Bowl 63

Seared Lemon Steak with Vegetables Stir-Fry 64

Vegetable Tabbouleh 65

Peppered Steak with Cherry Tomatoes...66

Grilled Chicken Breast with Non-Fat Yogurt 67
Delicious Low Fat Chicken Curry 68
Tilapia with Mushroom Sauce 69
Ginger Chicken with Veggies 70
Hot Lemon Prawns 71
Delicious Chicken Tikka Skewers 72
Grilled Chicken with Salad Wrap 73
MEAT RECIPES 74
Pork Casserole 75
Delicious Pork Roast Baracoa 75
Swedish Meatballs & Mushrooms Gravy 76
Cherry & Apple Pork 77
Paleo Italian Pork 78
Corned Pork 79
Chipotle Pork Carnitas 80
Slow Cooked Pork Tenderloin 81
Pork with Carrots & Apples 82
Shredded Pork Tacos 83
Pork Ragu with Tagliatelle 84
Pork with Olives & Feta 86
Bone in Ham with Maple-Honey Glaze 86
FISH RECIPES 88
Halibut with Fruit Salad 88
Poached Cod and Leeks 89
Cilantro Halibut with Coconut Milk 90
Easy Baked Cod 91
Herbed Salmon with Onions 92
Chinese Salmon 93
Spinach and Scallop 93
Crab Salad 94
Garlic Cod Soup 95
Chili Coconut Salmon 96
Clams with Olives Mix 97

SOUPS & STEW	99
Creamy Soup with Broccoli	99
Classic Soup with Butternut Squash	100
Thai Soup with Potato	101
Extraordinary Creamy Green Soup	102
Zingy Soup with Ginger, Carrot, and Lime	103
Native Asian Soup with Squash and Shitake	104
Peppery Soup with Tomato	105
Moroccan Inspired Lentil Soup	106
Classic Vegetarian Tagine	107
Homemade Warm and Chunky Chicken Soup	108
Indian Curried Stew with Lentil and Spinach	109
Soulful Roasted Vegetable Soup	110
Corn Chowder	111
Egg Drop Soup	112
SNACK RECIPES	114
Potato Sticks	114
Zucchini Chips	115
Spinach Chips	117
Sweet & Tangy Seeds Crackers	117
Plantain Chips	118
Quinoa & Seeds Crackers	119
Apple Leather	120
Roasted Cashews	121
Roasted Pumpkin Seeds	122
Spiced Popcorn	122
DESSERT RECIPES	124
Coconut and Seed Porridge	124
Pecan and Lime Cheesecake	125
Fluffy Chocolate Chip Cookies	126
Chewy Almond Blondies	127
Light Greek Cheesecake	128
Fluffy Chocolate Crepes	129

Crispy Peanut Fudge Squares	129
Almond Butter Cookies	130
Blueberry Cheesecake Bowl	131
SMOOTHIES RECIPES	133
Greek Yogurt Smoothie	133
Pineapple Smoothie	134
Blueberry Banana Smoothie	135
Blueberry Pie Smoothie	136
Strawberry Banana Smoothie	136
Mango Pineapple Smoothie	137
Avocado Smoothie	138
Strawberry Smoothie	138
Spinach Smoothie	140
Mint Chocolate Chip Smoothie	141
Chocolate Protein Smoothie	141
Peach Kiwi Green Smoothie	142
STAPLES, SAUCES AND DRESSINGS	144
Honey-Lime Vinaigrette with Fresh Herbs	145
Creamy Avocado Dressing	145
Avocado Crema	146
Romesco	147
Creamy Turmeric Dressing	148
Cherry-Peach Chutney with Mint	149
Tofu-Basil Sauce	150
Creamy Sesame Dressing	151
CONCLUTION	153

BASICS OF PANCREATITIS

As a consequence of trauma (such as gallstones), infection (such as influenza), hereditary factors, or alcoholism, the pancreas may become inflamed and develop pancreatitis (pancreatitis may develop in chronic alcoholics). One in ten adults over the age of 70 who have chronic pancreatitis has been given a diagnosis. It has been successful to treat chronic pancreatitis using pancreatic enzymes. It might cause agonizing agony and worsen obesity and malnutrition. Digestive enzymes and fats (lipases), which are produced by the pancreas, break down lipids and make them available to the cells for use as fuel.

Explanation of Pancreatitis

The pancreas is an organ in your body that is situated behind the stomach and small intestine. Its function includes making the enzymes necessary for your intestines to digest food. Through the pancreatic ducts, the enzymes are released from the pancreas and enter the small intestine's head as digestive juice.

At birth, the pancreatic divisum seems to be the most common defect. In human embryos, the pancreas is often split into two parts, each of which has the dorsal duct and the ventral duct. These two parts often combine throughout development, along with the two ducts, to create a single duct. During development, the ducts of the pancreas divisum cannot connect, maintaining the pancreas' two separate ducts.

Physiology of the Pancreas

The pancreas serves two major functions. It begins by creating chemical enzymes for digestion before releasing them into the small intestines. These enzymes break down carbohydrates, proteins, and lipids in food.

Additionally, the pancreas produces and releases hormones into the blood. One of these hormones, insulin, regulates the amount of sugar in the blood (glucose). Insulin also helps with energy production now and energy storage for the future.

Pancreatitis types

The three main types of pancreatitis are chronic pancreatitis, acute pancreatitis, and hereditary pancreatitis. But how do these three groups differ from one another, and how are they each treated? In this part, we'll go through the three basic types of pancreatitis and how to treat them.

Chronic vs. Acute

"Acute" or "chronic" is the main distinction between acute and chronic pancreatitis. Acute refers to a brief event, while chronic refers to a long-lasting or recurring event. After a few days, acute pancreatitis normally disappears. However, it typically requires IV fluids, antibiotics, or pain medication.

A more sophisticated treatment approach is required for chronic pancreatitis. Patients with chronic pancreatitis could need a lengthy hospital stay in order to manage their discomfort and obtain IV fluids. In the long term, patients may need to take an enzyme supplement in addition to changing their food habits. A piece of the pancreas may need to be removed if it has been seriously damaged.

Pancreatitis inherited

Hereditary pancreatitis is the term used to describe pancreatitis that affects family members. Hereditary pancreatitis may be acute or chronic. The initial stages of a diagnosis are often a physical examination and a review of the patient's medical history. A diagnosis may be made more specific with the use of diagnostic tests. Patients who have a family history of pancreatitis need more frequent and earlier screenings for the condition than other patients.

The severity of the issue determines the kind of treatment that is best for each patient.

Causes and Symptoms of Pancreatitis

The causes of pancreatitis and symptoms that point to the condition are listed below.

Causes

Gallstones or overindulging in alcohol are common causes of pancreatitis. Additional factors that might lead to pancreatitis include: Additional factors that might lead to pancreatitis include:

- Medications (some may irritate the pancreas);
- High triglyceride levels (fats in the blood);
- Infections
- Abdominal injuries
- Diabetes and other metabolic conditions
- Genetic diseases such as cystic fibrosis

Symptoms

Depending on the situation, pancreatitis may cause a variety of symptoms, including:

Acute pancreatitis symptoms

The following signs and symptoms of acute pancreatitis include:

- Extremely uncomfortable upper abdominal pain that might radiate to the back
- a sudden onset of pain or pain that gradually worsens over many days;
- a tender, bloated belly;
- common side symptoms including nausea and vomiting;
- a fever;
- an elevated heart rate.

Symptoms of chronic pancreatitis
The majority of the symptoms of chronic pancreatitis overlap with those of acute pancreatitis.

- A constant, sometimes paralyzing ache that travels from your neck to your back
- Unaccounted-for weight loss
- diabetic (high blood sugar) if the insulin-producing cells in the pancreas are damaged;
- foamy diarrhea with visible oil droplets (steatorrhea);

5 Steps of Pancreatitis Diet & Exercises

The prevention, diagnosis, and management of pancreatitis will all be covered in this chapter, along with some dos and don'ts.

Foods to Avoid While Having Pancreatitis

There are a few dietary modifications you may make when the pancreas divisum causes pancreatitis to lessen the incidence of flare-ups. The list of items that should be included in the diet is provided below.

- Some canned fish meat and white fish
- Vegetables
- Fruits
- tender flesh
- Skinless meat from poultry
- Beans and lentils
- Whole grains
- Sports drink
- Plant-based, non-fried food

Foods with Pancreatitis to Avoid

There are a few dietary modifications you may make when the pancreas divisum causes pancreatitis to lessen the incidence of flare-ups. The list of foods that should be cut back on or removed from the diet is provided below.

- Meat from organs
- Fried foods
- Prepared foods

- Full-fat dairy products
- Red meat:
- Alcohol
- Margarine or butter
- Desserts and sweets high in sugar
- A few nuts

Reduce the amount of fat you consume.

The overall amount of fat an individual needs depends on their height and weight. However, it is advised to keep total fat consumption to no more than 30% of daily caloric intake. 70 grams of fat is the maximum amount that someone who eats 2,000 calories per day should eat. 20 grams or less of saturated fat should be consumed daily.

Lean foods like fish and boneless, skinless chicken breasts often have minimal levels of saturated fat. Therefore, including them in your meal is a straightforward strategy to reduce the quantity of fat in your diet. On the other hand, some people's flare-ups may be triggered by high-protein diets. Before increasing the protein in your diet, talk to your doctor.

You may lose weight by cooking without butter and instead using cooking spray.

Limit your alcohol consumption and drink plenty of water.

Alcohol should never be consumed if you have pancreatic disease of any kind. Alcohol immediately damages and inflames the pancreas. Be hydrated since dehydration might cause pancreatic flare-ups as well. Always have a bottle of water or a non-alcoholic beverage with you. Sports drinks are a useful addition to your dehydration prevention arsenal.

Pancreatitis Attack Prevention Measures

Therapy is not required since the majority of people with pancreatic divisum do not exhibit any symptoms. Those who exhibit symptoms of this condition may find it challenging to decide on a course of treatment. Sphincterotomy or the Puestow procedure may be suggested by a surgeon. By removing the minor papilla, a hole that spans the small intestine and one of the ducts, they may widen the aperture between the two. A stent may be placed in the duct during surgery to prevent it from closing and obstructing. The best method to prevent pancreatitis is to have a healthy lifestyle. Maintain a healthy weight, engage in regular exercise, give up smoking, and abstain from alcohol.

By implementing these sensible lifestyle changes, acute pancreatitis instances resulting from gallstones, which cause 40% of cases, may be prevented. A gallbladder removal may be suggested by your doctor if you often have uncomfortable gallstones.

Yoga

Researchers have shown that persons with acute pancreatitis who practice yoga twice a week report improvements in their overall quality of life, anxiety symptoms, mood swings, alcohol dependence, and appetite.

Massage Treatment

Massage therapy involves using touch, different kneading techniques, or stroking the muscles of the body. It might be a full-body massage or a partial one. Massage may be applied to bare flesh or via clothing. It may be carried out at a table or on certain chairs. Only licensed massage therapists are permitted to provide massage therapy.

Massage improves circulation, reduces edema, soothes and relieves muscle and bone pain. It might be a stress reliever and an addition to other treatments. Research has shown that massage increases one's capacity for relaxation and general sense of wellbeing.

Physiological Contact

Using the fingers as a focal point to transmit energy, a therapist uses therapeutic touch to promote healing. It concentrates on the idea that people are energy. When we are healthy, our bodies' energy flows smoothly and is controlled. An imbalance or interruption in the energy flow is what causes the sickness.

Therapeutic touch sessions may take anywhere from 5 to 30 minutes, depending on the needs of the particular patient. Practitioners use a variety of methods, but in general, they move their hands from head to toe and over the front and back of the fully dressed subject while maintaining a distance of two to four inches. Studies have shown that therapeutic touch may increase tranquility, relaxation, and overall wellbeing. Studies have also demonstrated that therapeutic touch may change how people perceive pain and lessen stress.

Meditation

A state of peaceful, tension-free existence is encouraged through relaxation or meditation. To relax, a variety of techniques may be utilized, including guided or visual imagery, diaphragmatic breathing, muscular relaxation, repeating affirmations, prayer, and yoga. Daily meditation practice may improve concentration, sleep, and stress management. It may help with pain, anxiety, and stress management.

Laughter

Science is examining the effects of laughing that is "mirthful," or laughter that is motivated by pleasure rather than by negative emotions like guilt or concern. Although it goes without saying that laughing may elevate one's mood, multiple researchers are finding evidence that it may also strengthen one's immune system. To completely comprehend the positive effects of laughing, further research is required.

Acupuncture

The term "acupuncture" describes a collection of methods that include stimulating various anatomical places on the body. In the United States, acupuncture is influenced by medical traditions from Korea, China, Japan, and other countries. The acupuncture technique that has received the most scientific research involves inserting hard, thin metallic needles into the skin under manual or electrical control.

Treatment

If you get pancreatitis, your doctor will probably refer you to a consultant. A gastroenterologist should be in charge of your care (a specialist specializing in the digestive system).

- Treatment options for acute pancreatitis may include one or more of the following:
- In-patient treatment and supervision in a medical facility
- Painkillers that promote relaxation

A gallstone, another blockage, or a damaged section of the pancreas may be removed using an endoscopic approach or by surgery.

You may need extra pancreatic enzymes and insulin if your pancreas isn't functioning correctly.

Treatment Options for Pancreatitis

An endoscopic procedure is used to address the majority of pancreatitis problems, including pancreatic pseudocysts (inflammatory cysts) and impacted pancreatic tissue (inserting a tube down your throat until it reaches your small intestine, next to your pancreas). Gallstones and pancreatic stones are removed via endoscopic procedures.

If surgery is required, specialists can typically perform laparoscopic procedures. The surgical method has fewer, quicker-healing wounds.

During laparoscopic surgery, a laparoscope (a piece of apparatus with a tiny camera and light) is introduced via keyhole-sized incisions in the abdomen. The doctor may utilize the images of your organs provided by the laparoscope to guide them through the surgery.

Lifestyle Recommendations for Pancreatitis Patients

The left pancreas may not produce enough enzymes to aid in food digestion since a section of it was removed during surgery. As a result, patients may not be able to break down or metabolize the fats in their food. As undigested fat remains in the stools, it encourages diarrhea and poor nutrition. Possible adverse effects include bloating, increased gas output, and stomach pains. For these patients, controlling bloating, cramps, and gas as well as decreasing or eliminating diarrhea, reestablishing sufficient nutrition, avoiding weight loss, and managing diarrhea are all top considerations.

People who have had a Whipple procedure are more likely than those who have had a distal pancreatectomy to have insufficient enzyme production (another form of pancreatic surgery). Make the following lifestyle changes while you recover from pancreatitis:

- Take alternative pancreatic products at the recommended dosage with all meals and snacks.
- Eat six to eight small meals and snacks every day to prevent feeling bloated. More readily absorbed are smaller meals. There should be a 2-3 hour gap between meals.

- Sip drinks throughout meals in smaller doses. If a patient drinks too much liquid while eating, it might make them feel sick or make them throw up. A half hour before or after eating, drink water to avoid feeling full.
- Drinks containing vitamins, minerals, and protein are all excellent sources of calories. You may drink them in moderation during meals or substitute them for meals or snacks with protein smoothies or beverages that are nutritious supplements.
- After the procedure, maintain a daily dietary journal for the patient. Keep note of your daily weight, pancreatic enzyme use, bowel movements frequency and regularity, blood glucose levels, and other measurements in addition to the meals and quantities you eat (if applicable). This information may be utilized to monitor nutritional progress and help the doctor or dietician come up with further recommendations.

Drink Lots of Water

Everyone needs to stay hydrated for good health, but those with acute pancreatitis need it much more than normal. Few individuals with chronic pancreatitis recognize the need for proper hydration, although many recognize the value of limiting fat. Patients who are dehydrated experience breakouts (increased discomfort). The accumulation of pancreatic sludge is thought to be caused by a lack of fluid, although the exact origin is uncertain. The pancreas could then get inflamed as a result of blockages brought on by this sludge. Dehydration is often brought on by hot weather, large water deficits, flying, an increased activity level, and inadequate nourishment. It's important to keep in mind that thirst is a sign of dehydration rather than an accurate indicator of how much liquid we need. Any beverage without caffeine or alcohol may be utilized to satisfy the need for fluids. Because they are diuretics, promote fluid loss, and stimulate the pancreas, caffeine and alcohol should only be used in moderation. The need for fluids may also be satisfied by fruits, vegetables, and soups with a high water content. Remember that feeling thirsty is an indication of dehydration. Make sure to hydrate yourself before you get thirsty. What are your best choices? Always carry a bottle of water with you! Remember that on warmer days or days when you are exercising more, you may need more fluids.

Physical activity to hasten weight loss

More harmful than you would think are extra belly fat and waist fat. Obesity is usually linked to long-term conditions like type 2 diabetes. Recent research suggests that it could result in acute pancreatitis. Doctors believe that the excess abdominal fat of an obese individual may exacerbate acute pancreatitis. They observed that acute [sudden-onset] pancreatitis considerably damages abdominal fat, whereas diverticulitis [another cause of stomach pain] does not. The enzyme PNLIP is in charge of its degradation. This enzyme may encourage the formation of fatty acids, impairing the performance of vital physiological systems such as the circulatory, renal, and respiratory systems. The scientists believe that inhibiting PNLIP might prevent severe pancreatitis, reduce hospital stays, and even save lives.

For you to try, we've produced a list of some of the best exercises. There is no special equipment required for these exercises. All you need is a mat and some restraint.

Planks

Lay on your stomach and elevate yourself using your forearms and toes. Avoid drooping, and keep your posture strong and upright. Hold this position for 30 seconds. Ten seconds are added every week to the length.

Cycling crunches

Lay on your back with your legs extended and your hands on your ears. Next, raise your right knee until it touches your sternum. As you raise your upper body and turn to the right, bring your right knee and left elbow into alignment. Lower your body to go back to the starting position. On the other side, repeat the process with the left knee and right elbow. a rep for 15 sets in total. Increase the number of repetitions by five per week.

Get your legs up.

With your arms at your sides, lie on your back. Gradually raise your legs until they are 90 degrees off the ground. Without hitting the ground, lower your legs gradually. Return the legs to their original position and maintain it for a moment. Repeat this procedure 10 times in all. Each week, increase your rounds by two.

avian dogs

Kneel with your body on all fours and your arms out in front of you. Now stretch your left leg behind you and your right arm in front of you. For around two seconds, maintain this position with your hands. then return to your starting point. Repeat with the right leg and left arm. Repeat this procedure 20 times in all. Add 2 seconds to your position hold each week.

Jogging

Depending on your physical condition, you may begin jogging for 5 to 10 minutes twice a day. After speaking with your doctor, you can increase your activity to 45 minutes at least three times each week. It would be beneficial if nothing interrupted your training. It's time for you to look for yourself. If you are unable to walk, there are alternative methods of exercise (e.g., stretching, isometric exercises).

You won't need to spend hours at the gym if you do these exercises six days a week for a month. For best results, combine these exercises with portion control.

Sports

Abdominal fat is significantly impacted by physical exercise. Exercise helps to burn off extra calories, and it's especially helpful for getting rid of belly fat since it lowers levels of circulating insulin, which diminishes the body's propensity to store fat. Sports participation is a fun method to stay active, enhance cardiovascular fitness, reduce blood sugar levels, and lose weight instead of spending hours on the treadmill. To get the most metabolic bang for your buck, choose the most targeted exercises.

How the Pancreatitis Diet Differs from Other Diets

With so many weight-loss plans on the market, separating fact from fiction could be challenging. Investigators chose to try out three well-known diets in New Zealand. On weight loss, blood pressure lowering, and other parameters, the Mediterranean diet, intermittent fasting, and the paleo diet were compared. To find out how they contrast, keep reading. Let's first examine each diet in more detail on its own.

Superfood

Foods with the greatest nutritional value for the fewest calories are referred to as "superfoods." They are rich in vitamins, minerals, and antioxidants. Superfoods are foods that, based on their nutritional makeup, provide health benefits that go above and beyond what you might expect. Among the components are avocado, berries, salmon, green leafy vegetables, legumes, green tea, garlic, ginger, mushrooms, yogurt, almonds, and seeds.

A Paleo diet

A paleo diet is an eating regimen based on foods that were most likely eaten between 3 million and 10,000 years ago, during the Paleolithic epoch. A paleo diet often consists of foods that were once exclusively found via hunting and gathering, such as fish, lean meats, vegetables, fruits, seeds, and nuts. Around 10,000 years ago, when farming first started, a paleo diet excluded common foods. The food list includes grains, legumes, and dairy items.

Alternate-Day Fasting

A type of eating called intermittent fasting alternates between periods of eating and fasting. It gives you timing instructions rather than food recommendations. In this sense, it's more appropriately referred to as a dietary habit than a conventional diet. Two popular methods of intermittent fasting include fasting for 16 hours every day and fasting for 24 hours twice a week.

Pancreatitis diet

The best foods for chronic pancreatitis are whole grains, low-fat dairy, vegetables, fruits, legumes, and lean cuts of meat. Olive oil, almonds, avocados, fatty fish, and seeds are examples of healthy fats that may be taken in moderation. The Mediterranean diet and this one are fairly comparable.

Similarity and Dissimilarity Between the Pancreatitis Diet and Other Diets

The bulk of healthy eating techniques work under ideal conditions. Simply adhere to the directions, and presto! You'll look and feel better! On the other hand, reality isn't exactly pleasant. A study of actual eaters showed which healthy eating strategies work in real life.

Similarities between the Pancreatitis Diet and the Paleo Diet

The major commonalities are as follows: Both diets place an emphasis on whole, organic meals while eliminating processed foods and sugary drinks. Both diets place an emphasis on healthy fats, nuts, seeds, fruit, a wide variety of vegetables, and leafy greens.

The Pancreatitis Diet and Paleo: Differences and Similarities

a diet high in seafood and low in dairy, pork, and poultry for pancreatitis. Whole foods are prioritized in the Paleo diet above processed meals. This strict diet forbids grains and other cultivated foods (potatoes, legumes, etc.). The consumption of meat and poultry has grown.

The resemblance between the pancreatitis diet and intermittent fasting

Both diets include fruits, vegetables, nuts, whole grains, extra virgin olive oil, fish, and seafood. It limits a person's intake of red meat, dairy products, and eggs.

The Distinction Between the Pancreatitis Diet and Intermittent Fasting

The pancreatitis diet was mostly composed of fruits, vegetables, fish, and whole grains, with red meat and processed grains being strictly prohibited. A two-day limited fast was employed after a five-day unrestricted intermittent fasting regimen (commonly called 5:2).

Superfoods and the pancreatitis diet are comparable.

Berries, fruits, vegetables, and nut intake are emphasized in both diets.

Superfood vs. Pancreatitis Diet: Differences

Carrots, grapes, blueberries, walnuts, pomegranates, dark-green vegetables, red berries, and sweet potatoes are among the foods high in antioxidants that are beneficial for a pancreatitis diet. Olive oil, avocado, nuts, seeds, and fatty seafood should all be consumed in moderation.

BREAKFAST RECIPES

Salmon & Cucumber Toast

Preparation time: 5 minutes
Cooking time: 5 minutes
Servings: 2
Ingredients:

- 2 slices of whole grain bread
- 2 oz. Greek yogurt
- Salt & Pepper
- 1/4 red onion thinly sliced
- 4 oz. smoked salmon
- 1 cucumber, sliced

Directions:

1. Toast a piece of bread on a griddle or cook it on an electric grill. On one side of the piece of bread, spread Greek yogurt.
2. Place a piece of bread on top of the smoked salmon, cucumber, and onion. Sprinkle the top with salt and pepper. Dispense and savor!

Nutritional Info: Calories 222 Protein 20 g Carbohydrate 21 g Fats 5g

Pancakes Wraps

Preparation time: 5 minutes
Cooking time: 10 minutes
Servings: 6

Ingredients:

- 1 1/4 cup spelt flour
- 1/4 tsp. salt
- ¼ tsp. baking powder
- 6 eggs
- 1 cup almond milk
- 1 banana sliced
- chocolate syrup
- 2 oz. Greek yogurt

Directions:

1. In a bowl, combine flour, salt, and baking powder. In another dish, whisk milk and eggs until well combined. Mix thoroughly after adding the egg and milk combination to the flour mixture.

2. Spray a griddle with nonstick cooking spray, heat it over medium heat, then pour and distribute 1/4 cup of pancake batter on it.

3. Cook the pancake for two to three minutes on each side, or until the top bubbles pop and leave little holes. Cooked food should be removed from the griddle.

4. Cover the pancake with low-fat Greek yogurt and fold it. Add a piece of banana and chocolate syrup on top.

Nutritional Info: Calories 226 Protein 13 g Carbohydrate 27 g Fats 8 g

Cinnamon Glazed Waffle Rolls

Preparation time: 5 minutes
Cooking time: 10 minutes
Servings: 2
Ingredients:

- 4 eggs
- 1/2 cup oat flour
- 1 tsp cinnamon

Cinnamon roll glaze:

- 2 tbsps. Greek yogurt
- 1 tsp. cinnamon
- 1/2 banana

Directions:

1. Turn the circular waffle maker on and let it preheat. In a bowl, combine all the waffle ingredients. Waffle makers should be greased with nonstick frying spray.
2. Fill a greased waffle machine with the waffle batter. Waffles should be cooked for 3 to 4 minutes after the waffle maker is closed.
3. After being cooked, remove the waffles from the waffle machine. In a dish, combine the glaze's components. Roll up the waffles after glazing them. Dispense and savor!

Nutritional Info: Calories 237 Protein 14 g Carbohydrate 19 g Fats 10 g

Spinach & Quinoa Muffins

Preparation time: 20 minutes
Cooking time: 20 minutes
Servings: 8
Ingredients:

- 2 cups spinach finely chopped
- 1 tbsps. oregano

- 8 eggs
- 1 cup cooked quinoa
- 1 cup buckwheat flour
- ¼ cup almond milk
- 1 tsp. baking powder
- 1/4 tsp. salt

Directions:

1. Set the oven temperature to 350 degrees. In a bowl, whisk the eggs with the milk and oregano. Mix thoroughly after adding the other ingredients to the egg mixture.
2. Fill muffin pans with batter, oil them, and bake the muffins for 15-20 minutes, or until they are lightly golden brown.
3. Remove the baked muffins from the oven. Dispense and savor!

Nutritional Info: Calories 154 Protein 9 Carbohydrate 17 g Fats 5 g

Overnight Oat Pudding Jar

Preparation time: 10 minutes
Cooking time: 0 minutes
Servings: 2

Ingredients:

- banana
- 3/4 cup almond milk
- Pinch sea salt
- 1 cup rolled oats
- 1 1/2 tbsps. chia seeds
- 1 cup strawberries sliced

Directions:

1. In a blender, combine the banana, almond milk, and sea salt. Process until the mixture is smooth.
2. Pour the mixture over the oats and chia seeds in a glass container, then stir to combine. Cover and chill overnight.
3. Remix in the morning and, if necessary, add extra almond milk. Serve with sliced fresh strawberries on top, and enjoy.

Nutritional Info: Calories 233 Protein 10 g Carbohydrate 51 g Fats 7 g

Zucchini & Chickpeas Frittata

Preparation time: 10 minutes
Cooking time: 20 minutes
Servings: 4

Ingredients:

- 1 cup almond milk
- 1 cup chickpeas flour
- 1 tsp. dried oregano
- salt and pepper, to taste
- 4 -6 baby zucchini
- 1 tsp. baking powder
- 4-5 zucchini flowers
- ½ cup thinly sliced red onion

Directions:

1. Heat some oil in a nonstick pan. In an oiled skillet, add the onion and simmer for two to three minutes. In a bowl, add the zucchini.
2. In a bowl, combine the chickpeas, milk, baking powder, salt, pepper, and oregano. Put the zucchini blossoms on top of the batter before adding the onion and zucchini.

3. Cook the frittata in a preheated oven for 20 to 30 minutes, or until fully done. Please serve hot.
Nutritional Info: Calories 177 Protein 9 g Carbohydrate 24 g Fats 5 g

Oat Pudding with Chia Seeds

Preparation time: 10 minutes
Cooking time: 0 minutes
Servings: 2
Ingredients:

- 1/2 cup Oats rolled oats
- 1 tbsp. chia seeds
- 1 cup almond milk
- pinch of salt
- 1 cup strawberries
- yogurt for topping
- berries for topping
- walnuts for topping

Directions:

1. Fill a glass jar with a lid and add the dates, milk, oats, seeds, and salt. jar in the refrigerator for the night.
2. Fill the serving jar with the oat mixture and add the strawberries to the top. Oats, strawberries, and chopped walnuts go on top. Dispense and savor!

Nutritional Info: Calories 122 Protein 6 g Carbohydrate 22 g Fats 5 g

Quick & Easy Shakshuka

Preparation time: 10 minutes
Cooking time: 20 minutes
Servings: 2
Ingredients:

- 1 onion finely sliced
- 2 red bell peppers finely sliced
- 2 cups tomatoes, chopped
- 1 tsp. spicy harissa
- 4 eggs
- 1 tbsp. chopped parsley
- Salt and pepper to taste

Directions:
1. Add onions and peppers to a pan that has been greased with nonstick cooking spray, and cook for 4–5 minutes, or until tender. Cook the tomatoes and harissa in the skillet for a further 3–4 minutes.
2. Sprinkle salt and pepper on top and thoroughly combine. eggs are cracked over tomatoes. Cook pan with lid on until egg whites are just starting to set.
3. Sprinkle freshly chopped parsley on top and serve right away with a piece of whole grain bread. Enjoy.

Nutritional Info: Calories 182 Protein 13 g Carbohydrate 13 g Fats 8 g

Scramble Egg Whites Wrap

Preparation time: 5 minutes

Cooking time: 15 minutes
Servings: 2
Ingredients:

- 1 cup eggs whites, cooked, scrambled
- 1 cup hummus
- ½ cup sweet corn, boiled
- salt and pepper to taste
- 2 homemade corn tortillas

Directions:

1. Cook egg whites with salt and pepper in a nonstick skillet over medium heat for 2–3 minutes.
2. Spoon scrambled eggs onto each tortilla in equal portions. Add corn and hummus on top.
3. Fold the tortilla and reheat it on a hot griddle for 2 to 3 minutes. Slice, then serve right away. Enjoy!

Nutritional Info: Calories 365 Protein 21 g Carbohydrate 51 g Fats 8 g

Asparagus & Tomato Omelet

Preparation time: 5 minutes
Cooking time: 15 minutes
Servings: 2
Ingredients:

- salt & black pepper to taste
- 4 large eggs
- 5 -6 stalks asparagus, trimmed
- 2-3 tomatoes

- Chopped parsley for topping
- Chopped scallion for topping

Directions:

1. In a nonstick pan, heat the oil over medium heat. Asparagus should be added to a hot skillet and cooked for 2-4 minutes. until the asparagus is tender and has a deep green hue.
2. Season with salt and pepper and pour beaten eggs over asparagus.Eggs should be cooked for around 4–5 minutes under a cover.
3. Top with onion, tomato, and parsley. Enjoy after serving.

Nutritional Info: Calories 193 Protein 15 g Carbohydrate 11 g Fats 10 g

Fluffy Pancakes

Preparation time: 10 minutes
Cooking time: 15 minutes
Servings: 2

Ingredients:

- 1 cup oat flour
- 4 large eggs
- 1 tsp. baking powder

Topping:

- coconut cream for topping
- cashew nuts for topping
- strawberry puree for topping

Directions:

1. In a bowl, combine all the pancake ingredients and stir until the batter is smooth and fluffy. Grease a skillet with cooking spray and heat it over medium heat.
2. Spoon 1/4 cup pancake batter into a buttered pan and smooth it out just a little. Pancakes should be flipped over and cooked for two to three minutes on each side, until just beginning to brown.
3. Remove from the pan and top with strawberry jam, cashews, and coconut cream. Enjoy!

Nutritional Info: Calories 373 Protein 21 g Carbohydrate 36 g Fats 15 g

Kale & Quinoa Breakfast Bowl

Preparation time: 10 minutes
Cooking time: 15 minutes
Servings: 2
Ingredients:

- 1 tsp. onion powder
- ½ tsp. salt
- ½ tsp. pepper
- 1 bag baby kale
- 1 cup chickpeas boiled
- 1 cup cooked quinoa
- 1 carrot, sliced and steamed
- 1 tsp. sesame seeds

Directions:

1. In a bowl, combine chickpeas, quinoa, and carrots. Pour oil, salt, pepper, and onion powder over the chickpeas in the bowl.
2. Top with sesame seeds. Enjoy it when serving it with greens!

Nutritional Info: Calories 224 Protein 10 g Carbohydrate 38 g Fats 4 g

Muesli Breakfast Bowl With Berries

Preparation time: 10 minutes
Cooking time: 0 minutes
Servings:2
Ingredients:

- 1 cup muesli
- 2/3 cup almond milk
- 1/4 cup blueberries
- 1 apple sliced with skin
- 1 oz. roasted pumpkin seeds

Directions:
1. Stir the milk into the muesli in a medium bowl until it is tender and soft.
2. Add a piece of apple, blueberries, pumpkin seeds, or any other fruit to soft muesli. Enjoy!

Nutritional Info: Calories 320 Protein 14 g, Carbohydrate 57 g, Fats 13 g

Greek Yogurt with Fig Mulberries Pumpkin Seed

Preparation time: 10 minutes
Cooking time: 0 minutes
Servings: 2
Ingredients:

- 8 oz. fresh figs, halved
- 1 cup low fat Greek yogurt
- 1 oz. pumpkin seeds
- 2 oz. mulberries

Directions:

1. In a medium bowl, combine the milk and muesli and stir until smooth and creamy.
2. To soft muesli, add an apple slice, blueberries, pumpkin seeds, or any other fruit. Enjoy!

Nutritional Info: Calories 351 Protein 17 g Carbohydrate 58 g Fats 7 g

Sweet Potato Omelet Pie

Preparation time: 10 minutes
Cooking time: 20 minutes
Servings: 6
Ingredients:

- 2 sweet potatoes, peeled and sliced into ¼ inch rounds
- 1 onion, sliced
- 10 eggs
- salt and pepper, to taste

Directions:

1. Melt butter over medium heat in a cast-iron ovenproof skillet. Add the sliced potatoes and simmer for a further 8 to 10 minutes, adding water as needed, until tender.
2. Add the onions and salt and pepper to taste. In a bowl, whisk

eggs with salt and pepper.

3. Spoon the beaten egg mixture over the potatoes, cover, and simmer for 5–8 minutes, or bake for 20 minutes in a preheated oven, until the eggs are done.

4. Remove from the oven when golden. Please serve hot.

Nutritional Info: Calories 146 Protein 10 g Carbohydrate 10 g Fats 7 g

LUNCH RECIPES

Vegan Baked Navy Beans

Preparation time: 15 minutes, plus 8 hours to soak
Cooking time: 7 to 8 hours on low
Serving: 4–6
Ingredients:

- 2 cups dried navy beans, soaked in water overnight, drained, and rinsed
- 6 cups vegetable broth
- ¼ cups dried cranberries
- 1 medium sweet onion, diced
- ½ cups all-natural ketchup (choose the one with the lowest amount of sugar)
- 3 tbsp. extra-virgin olive oil
- 2 tbsp. maple syrup
- 2 tbsp. molasses
- 1 tbsp. apple cider vinegar
- 1 tsp. Dijon mustard
- 1 tsp. sea salt
- ½ tsp. garlic powder

Directions:

1. Put the beans, broth, cranberries, onions, ketchup, maple syrup, molasses, vinegar, mustard, salt, and garlic powder in your slow cooker.
2. Set the cooker to low and cover it. Serve after cooking for 7 to 8 hours.

Nutritional Info: Calories: 423 Fat: 11 g. Carbs : 78 g. Protein: 16 g.

Hatch Chile "Refried" Beans

Preparation time: 15 minutes, plus 8 hours to soak
Cooking time: 6 to 8 hours on low
Serving: 4–6
Ingredients:

- 2 cups dried pinto beans, soaked in water overnight, drained, and rinsed
- 7 cups vegetable broth
- ½ medium onion, minced
- 1 (4-ounce) can Hatch green chilies
- 1 tsp. freshly squeezed lime juice
- ½ tsp. ground cumin
- ½ tsp. garlic powder
- ½ tsp. sea salt

Directions:

1. Combine the beans, broth, onion, chiles, lime juice, cumin, garlic powder, and salt in your slow cooker.
2. Set the cooker to low and cover it. Cook the beans for 6 to 8 hours, or until they are tender.
3. Before serving, puree the beans with an immersion blender to the desired smoothness. Use a fork or a potato masher to manually mash the beans if you don't have an immersion blender.

Nutritional Info: Calories: 218 Fat: 0 g.Carbs: 49 g.Protein: 16 g.

Indian Butter Chickpeas

Preparation time: 15 minutes, plus 8 hours to soak
Cooking time: 6 to 8 hours on low
Serving: 4–6

Ingredients:

- 1 tbsp. coconut oil
- 1 medium onion, diced
- 1-pound dried chickpeas, soaked in water overnight, drained, and rinsed
- 2 cups full-fat coconut milk
- 1 (14.5-ounce) can crushed tomatoes
- 2 tbsp. almond butter
- 2 tbsp. curry powder
- 1½ tsp. garlic powder
- 1 tsp. ground ginger
- ½ tsp. sea salt
- ½ tsp. ground cumin
- ½ tsp. chili powder

DIRECTION:

1. Rub coconut oil all over the slow cooker. The slow cooker's bottom should be covered in layers of onions.
2. Add the curry powder, garlic powder, ginger, salt, cumin, and chili powder along with the tomatoes, coconut milk, almond butter, and chickpeas. Stir slowly to incorporate the spices into the liquid.
3. Set the cooker to low and cover it. Cook the chickpeas for 6 to 8 hours, or until they are soft, and then serve.

Nutritional Info: Calories: 720 Fat: 30 g. Carbs: 86 g. Protein: 27 g.

Mediterranean Quinoa With Pepperoncini

Preparation time: 15 minutes or fewer
Cooking time: 6 to 8 hours on low
Serving: 4–6
Ingredients:

- 1½ cup quinoa, rinsed well
- 3 cups vegetable broth
- ½ tsp. sea salt
- ½ tsp. garlic powder
- ¼ tsp. dried oregano
- ¼ tsp. dried basil leaves
- Freshly ground black pepper
- 3 cups arugula
- ½ cup diced tomatoes
- 1/3 cup sliced pepperoncini
- ¼ cup freshly squeezed lemon juice
- 3 tbsp. extra-virgin olive oil

DIRECTION:
1. Combine the quinoa, broth, salt, oregano, basil, garlic powder, and pepper in your slow cooker. Set the cooker to low and cover it. For 6 to 8 hours, cook.
2. Combine the arugula, tomatoes, pepperoncini, lemon juice, and olive oil in a big bowl.
3. After the quinoa has finished cooking, combine it with the arugula salad before serving.

Nutritional Info: Calories: 359 Fat: 14 g. Carbs: 50 g. Protein: 10 g.

Coco-Nutty Brown Rice

Preparation time: 15 minutes, plus 8 hours to soak
Cooking time: 3 hours on high
Serving: 4–6
Ingredients:

- 2 cups brown rice, soaked in water overnight, drained, and rinsed
- 3 cups water
- 1½ cup full-fat coconut milk
- 1 tsp. sea salt
- ½ tsp. ground ginger
- Freshly ground black pepper

Directions:

1. Combine the rice, water, coconut milk, salt, and ginger in your slow cooker. Add pepper and mix the ingredients together.
2. Set the cooker to high and cover it. Serve after 3 hours of cooking.

Nutritional Info: Calories: 479 Fat: 19 g. Carbs: 73 g. Protein: 9 g.

Herbed Harvest Rice

Preparation time: 15 minutes, plus 8 hours to soak
Cooking time: 3 hours on high
Serving: 4–6
Ingredients:

- 2 cups brown rice, soaked in water overnight, drained, and rinsed

- ½ small onion, chopped
- 4 cups vegetable broth
- 2 tbsp. extra-virgin olive oil
- ½ tsp. dried thyme leaves
- ½ tsp. garlic powder
- ½ cups cooked sliced mushrooms
- ½ cups dried cranberries
- ½ cup toasted pecans

Directions:

1. Combine the rice, onion, broth, olive oil, thyme, and garlic powder in your slow cooker. Good stirring Set the cooker to high and cover it for three hours.
2. Add the pecans, cranberries, and mushrooms, and serve.

Nutritional Info: Calories: 546 Fat: 20 g. Carbs: 88 g. Protein: 10 g.

Veggie "Fried" Quinoa

Preparation time: 15 minutes or fewer
Cooking time: 4 to 6 hours on low
Serving: 4–6
Ingredients:

- 2 cups quinoa, rinsed well
- 4 cups vegetable broth
- ¼ cups sliced carrots
- ¼ cups corn kernels
- ¼ cups green peas
- ¼ cups diced scallion
- 1 tbsp. sesame oil
- 1 tbsp. garlic powder
- 1 tsp. sea salt

- Dash red pepper flakes

Directions:

1. Put the quinoa, broth, carrots, corn, peas, scallions, sesame oil, garlic powder, salt, and red pepper flakes in the slow cooker.
2. Set the cooker to low and cover it. Fluff after 4 to 6 hours of cooking and serve.

Nutritional Info: Calories: 387 Fat: 8 g. Carbs: 65 g. Protein: 13 g.

Chicken Salad Delight

Preparation time: 30 minutes
Cooking time: 5 minutes
Serving: 5
Ingredients:

- 2 cups diced chicken, fat and skin removed
- 1/2 cups plain, non-fat yogurt
- 1/2 cups celery, finely chopped
- 1/4 tsp. black pepper
- 1/4 cups onion, chopped
- 1/4 cups green pepper, chopped
- 1 tsp. dried parsley
- 1 tbsp. lemon juice
- 1 tsp. dry mustard
- 3 cups water

Directions:

1. Boil the chicken for 3–5 minutes on high heat in a saucepan with 3 cups of water. Remove extra water, then let it cool.
2. Combine the celery, green pepper, onion, and parsley in a large

mixing dish. Add the chicken, then stir in the lemon juice.
3. Combine the yogurt, mustard, and black pepper in another bowl. Mix the chicken mixture well after adding the dry ingredients. Lastly, add the lemon juice and combine once more. consume right away.

Nutritional Info: Calories: 181 Carbs: 3 g Protein: 18 g Fat: 10 g

Parsley Burger

Preparation time: 1 hour
Cooking time: 20 minutes
Serving: 4
Ingredients:

- 1 lb. ground beef
- 1 tbsp. lemon juice
- 1/4 tsp. oregano
- 1/4 tsp. ground thyme
- 1 tbsp. parsley flakes
- 1/4 tsp. black pepper
- Vegetable oil, for greasing

Directions:

1. Combine the meat, lemon juice, thyme, oregano, black pepper, and parsley flakes in a large mixing bowl. Mix each component well.
2. Create 4 tiny patties, each approximately 3/4 inch thick. Place the patties on a skillet or broiler pan that has been greased with vegetable oil. For 15 to 20 minutes, broil over medium-low heat.

Nutritional Info: Calories: 171 Carbs: 0 g. Protein: 20 g. Fat: 10 g.

Seasoned Pork Chops

Preparation time: 20 minutes
Cooking time: 50 minutes
Serving: 4
Ingredients:

- 4 4-oz lean pork chops, skin and fat removed
- 1/4 cup all-purpose white flour
- 1 tsp. black pepper
- 1/2 tsp. thyme
- 2 tbsp. canola oil
- 1/2 tsp. sage

Directions:

1. Turn the oven's temperature up to 350 degrees Fahrenheit. Grease a baking dish with a little canola oil.
2. Combine the flour, sage, thyme, and black pepper in a medium mixing bowl. Completely combine.
3. Place each pork chop in a greased pan after dredging it in the flour mixture. Cook for 40 to 50 minutes, or until golden and tender, in the oven. Serve.

Nutritional Info: Calories: 342 Carbs: 12 g. Protein: 19 g. Fat: 23 g.

Taco Stuffing

Preparation time: 30 minutes
Cooking time: 20 minutes
Serving: 8
Ingredients:

- 1 1/4 lb. ground beef or turkey

- 2 tbsp. canola oil
- 1/2 tsp. ground red pepper
- 1/2 tsp. nutmeg
- 1/2 tsp. black pepper
- 1/2 tsp. Tabasco sauce
- 1 tsp. Italian seasoning
- 1 tsp. garlic powder
- 1 tsp. onion powder

To serve:

- Lettuce
- Taco shells

Directions:

1. In a pan, heat the oil over medium heat before adding the ground beef and other ingredients. Cook for 15 to 20 minutes, or until the meat is cooked and the mixture is well combined.
2. Place lettuce shredded on top of each taco shell after adding 2 ounces of the beef mixture.

Nutritional Info: Calories: 176 Carbs: 9 g. Protein: 14 g. Fat: 9 g.

Jalapeno Popper Chicken

Preparation time: 5 minutes
Cooking time: 30 minutes
Serving: 8
Ingredients:

- 3 tbsp. vegetable oil
- 2 tsp. fresh jalapeno peppers, seeded, finely chopped

- 2–3 lbs. chicken, cut and fat and skin removed
- 1/4 tsp. black pepper
- 1 onion, sliced into rings
- 1/2 tsp. ground nutmeg
- 1 ½ cup chicken bouillon, made from lean chicken

Directions:

1. In a pan, heat the oil over medium heat. Add the chicken and cook it until it turns golden.
2. After a minute of sautéing, add the onion rings and bouillon. Regularly stir the liquid while you bring it to a boil.
3. Include nutmeg and black pepper. The chicken should be soft and tender after 25 to 30 minutes of simmering with the lid on the pan.
4. Add the jalapeno peppers and cook for an additional two minutes.

Nutritional Info: Calories: 143 Carbs: 2 g. Protein: 17 g. Fat: 7 g.

Tuna Au Poivre

Preparation time: 30 minutes
Cooking time: 10 minutes
Serving: 4
Ingredients:

- 1 tbsp. finely grated lemon zest
- 3–4 tsp. coarsely ground black pepper
- 2 garlic cloves, finely minced
- 2 tsp. dried oregano
- 1 tsp. kosher salt
- 4 6-ounce tuna
- Steaks 2 tsp.
- Olive oil 1 lemon, quartered

Directions:

1. On a sizable plate, combine the salt, oregano, black pepper, and lemon zest. Put the tuna through the mixture on both sides.
2. Heat up a sizable cast-iron skillet over medium-high heat before adding the oil. After about 5 minutes on each side, add the tuna and brown it.
3. Garnish with the lemon quarters before serving.

Nutritional Info: Calories: 305 Fat: 11 g.Carbs: 4 g.Protein: 45 g.

Fish Stew

Preparation time: 30 minutes
Cooking time: 55 minutes
Serving: 8
Ingredients:

- 2 tsp. olive oil
- 3 leeks, well washed, white, and light green parts only, or 1 Spanish onion, chopped
- 2 celery stalks, diced
- 2 carrots, diced peeled
- 1 fennel bulb, tough outer layers removed, trimmed, and diced
- 4 garlic cloves, finely chopped, or pressed
- 1/4 tsp. crushed red pepper
- 2 tsp. dried thyme
- 1 bay leaf
- 1/4 tsp. cayenne pepper
- 1/8 tsp. crushed saffron threads

- 1 28 ounce can whole tomatoes, chopped, including liquid
- 6 cups light fish broth or non-fat chicken broth
- 1 cup dry white wine
- Strips of zest from one orange
- 1-pound cod, cubed
- 1-pound halibut, cubed

Directions:

1. Heat up a sizable skillet on low heat, then add the olive oil once it is heated. Add the vegetables and simmer for approximately 10 minutes, or until the onion is golden.

2. Cook for 5 minutes before adding the garlic, herbs, and spices. Cook for 20 to 25 minutes after adding the tomatoes, fish broth, wine, and orange zest.

3. Increase the temperature to a high setting and bring the mixture to a boil. Cod and halibut should be added, and the heat should be reduced to low; cook for 10-15 minutes, or until the fish begins to come apart.

4. Pour 2 cups of the soup into a blender and mix until completely smooth. Come back to the soup.

5. Either serve right away or cover and keep chilled for up to two days. Serve with French bread toasts, croutons, and lemon wedges.

Nutritional Info: Calories: 185 Fat: 4 g. Carbs: 10 g. Protein: 27 g.

Grilled Salmon With Fruit And Sesame Vinaigrette

Preparation time: 15 minutes
Cooking time: 10 minutes

Serving: 4

Ingredients:

- 4 6-ounce salmon steaks
- 1 tsp. Kosher salt
- 1 tsp. black pepper
- 1 tsp. olive oil
- 1 garlic clove, crushed
- 1 tsp. finely chopped fresh ginger root peeled
- ½ cup chopped red onion
- 2 tbsp. sesame seeds
- 1/4 cup lemon or lime juice
- ¼ cup orange, apple, or pineapple juice
- ¼ tsp. white sugar
- 1 tbsp. balsamic vinegar
- 1 tbsp. finely chopped fresh basil or cilantro leaves
- 2 scallion greens, finely chopped
- ¼–½ tsp. kosher salt

Directions:

1. Get the grill or the broiler ready.
2. Add some salt and pepper to the fish. Place the steaks on the grill once it is hot, and cook them for 5 to 6 minutes on each side. Or you might put it under the broiler.
3. In the meantime, heat the oil in a large pan over medium-high heat.
4. Add the sesame seeds, garlic, ginger root, and onion, and simmer for approximately 5 minutes, or until the veggies are soft and the seeds are just beginning to brown.
5. Once the heat has been turned off, mix in the juices, sugar, vinegar, basil or cilantro, scallion greens, salt, and pepper. Add the

vinaigrette on top of the steaks when they are done. Serve right away.

Nutritional Info: Calories: 380 Fat: 207 Fat: 23 g. Carbs: 7 g.Protein: 35 g.

BASIC RECIPES

Minty Melon with Vinegar

Preparation Time: 5 minutes
Cooking time: 0 minutes
Servings: 4
Ingredients:
Dressing:

- 3 tablespoons olive oil
- 2 tablespoons red wine vinegar
- Sea salt, to taste

Salad:

- 1 honeydew melon, rind removed, flesh cut into 1-inch cubes
- ½ cantaloupe, rind removed, flesh cut into 1-inch cubes
- 3 stalks celery, sliced
- ½ red onion, thinly sliced
- ¼ cup chopped fresh mint

Directions:
Creating the Dressing 1. Combine the red wine vinegar and olive oil in a small bowl. Set it aside after seasoning it with sea salt.
Produce the salad.
2. Combine the honeydew, cantaloupe, celery, red onion, and mint in a big bowl.

3. Include the dressing and blend by tossing.

Nutritional Info: Calories: 223 Fat: 11g Protein: 2g Carbs: 32g

Mixed Greens Salad with Honeyed Dressing

Preparation Time: 10 minutes
Cooking time: 0 minutes
Servings: 4
Ingredients:
Dressing:

- ½ cup pitted Rainier cherries
- ¼ cup olive oil
- 2 tablespoons freshly squeezed lemon juice
- 2 tablespoons raw honey
- 1 teaspoon chopped fresh basil
- Pinch sea salt

Salad:

- 4 cups lightly blanched broccoli florets
- 2 cups mixed greens
- 1 cup snow peas
- ½ English cucumber, quartered lengthwise and sliced
- ½ red onion, thinly sliced

Directions:
Creating the Dressing 1. Blend the cherries, olive oil, lemon juice, honey, and basil together in a blender. Pulse until smooth. Set it aside after seasoning it with sea salt.

Produce the salad. 2. Combine the dressing with the broccoli, greens, snow peas, cucumber, and red onion in a large bowl and toss to combine.

Nutritional Info: Calories: 189 Fat: 13g Protein: 3g Carbs: 18g

Apricot Salad with Mustardy Dressing

Preparation Time: 10 minutes
Cooking time: 0 minutes
Servings: 4
Ingredients:
Dressing:

- ¼ cup olive oil
- 2 tablespoons balsamic vinegar
- 2 teaspoons whole-grain Dijon mustard
- 1 teaspoon chopped fresh thyme
- Sea salt, to taste

Salad:

- 4 cups mixed greens
- 1 cup arugula
- ½ red onion, thinly sliced
- 16 ounces (454 g) cooked turkey breast, chopped
- 3 apricots, pitted and each fruit cut into 8 pieces
- ½ cup chopped pecans

Directions:
Creation the dressing 1. Combine the olive oil, balsamic vinegar, mustard, and thyme in a small bowl. Set it aside after seasoning it

with sea salt

Produce the salad.

2. Combine the mixed greens, arugula, and red onion in a large bowl with 3/4 of the dressing. Place the salad on a serving plate after dressing it.

3. Add the turkey, apricots, and pecans to the greens. Serve with the remaining dressing drizzled on top.

Nutritional Info: Calories: 305 Fat: 20g Protein: 21g Carbs: 12g

Potato Caraway with Lemony Fillet

Preparation Time: 10 minutes
Cooking time: 15 minutes
Servings: 2
Ingredients:

- 1 cup peeled sweet potatoes
- 12 ounces (340 g) smoked mackerel fillets, skin removed
- 2 green onions, finely sliced
- 1 cup cooked beetroot, sliced into wedges
- 2 tablespoons finely chopped dill
- 2 tablespoons olive oil
- Juice of 1 lemon, zest of half
- 1 teaspoon crushed caraway seeds

Directions:

1. Boil the potatoes for one minute in a small saucepan, then simmer them for another 15 minutes over medium-high heat, or until they are tender to the fork. Slices should be thick and cool.

2. Add the chilled potatoes, green onions, beetroot, and dill to a bowl with the flaked mackerel.
3. Combine the olive oil, lemon juice, caraway seeds, and black pepper in another bowl.
4. Pour over the salad, then thoroughly toss to combine. Sprinkle the lemon zest on top. Refrigerate in plastic containers for later enjoyment or consume immediately.

Nutritional Info: Calories: 530 Fat: 38g Protein: 34g Carbs: 13g

Vinegary Berry with Orange Salad

Preparation Time: 10 minutes
Cooking time: 0 minutes
Servings: 1
Ingredients:

- 1 cup fresh spinach, leaves trimmed and coarsely chopped
- 1 orange, peeled and sliced
- 1 cup chopped fresh cranberries
- 2 tablespoons red wine vinegar
- 4 teaspoons olive oil
- 2 teaspoons peeled and grated ginger
- 1 pinch of black pepper

Directions:
1. In a salad bowl, whisk together the vinegar and olive oil. Add the cranberries, ginger, and pepper to taste.
2. Add the orange slices and spinach to the dressing, tossing to combine. Before serving, chill.

Nutritional Info: Calories: 298 Fat: 18g Protein: 2g Carbs: 32g

Cucumber and Spinach with Chicken Salad

Preparation Time: 10 minutes
Cooking time: 15 minutes
Servings: 2
Ingredients:

- 1 tablespoon extra-virgin olive oil
- 2 skinless chicken breasts, chopped
- 2 carrots, sliced
- ½ large onion, chopped
- 2 teaspoons cumin seeds
- ½ avocado, chopped
- 1 lime, juiced
- ½ cucumber, chopped
- ½ cup fresh spinach
- 1 mason jar

Directions:

1. Heat the oil in a skillet over medium heat before browning and cooking the chicken for 10 to 15 minutes. Remove from the oven and set aside to cool.
2. Include the onion and carrots and cook for an additional 5 to 10 minutes, or until soft.
3. Pack everything into the jar by first adding half of the avocado-lime mixture, then the cumin-roasted vegetables, and then the chicken.
4. Add the cilantro, spinach, tomatoes, and cucumbers on top, then chill for 20 minutes before serving.

Nutritional Info: Calories: 522 Fat: 22g Protein: 64g Carbs: 17g

Lemony Zucchini with Vinegary Salmon

Preparation Time: 10 minutes
Cooking time: 14 minutes
Servings: 2
Ingredients:

- 2 skinless salmon fillets
- 2 cups seasonal greens
- ½ cup sliced zucchini
- 1 tablespoon balsamic vinegar
- 2 tablespoons extra-virgin olive oil
- 2 sprigs thyme, torn from the stem
- 1 lemon, juiced

Directions:
1. Turn the broiler on to medium-high. For 10 minutes, broil the salmon wrapped in parchment paper with some oil, lemon, and pepper.
2. Slice the zucchini, add the oil to a skillet, and cook for 4 to 5 minutes.
3. Lay down a bed of zucchini and top with flakes of salmon to assemble the salad. Add a balsamic vinegar drizzle and some thyme.
Nutritional Info: Calories: 531 Fat: 27g Protein: 67g Carbs: 5g

Milky Carrot with Oniony Ginger Soup

Preparation Time: 5 minutes
Cooking time: 28 minutes
Servings: 6-8

Ingredients:

- 4½ cups plus 2 tablespoons water, divided
- 1 large onion, peeled and roughly chopped
- 8 carrots, peeled and roughly chopped
- 1½-inch piece fresh ginger, sliced thin
- 1¼ teaspoons sea salt
- 2 cups unsweetened coconut milk

Directions:

1. In a large saucepan, add 2 tablespoons of water, add the onion, and cook for 4 minutes or until transparent.
2. Fill the saucepan with the remaining water, salt, and carrots. After bringing the mixture to a boil, turn down the heat. For 20 minutes, simmer with a cover on.
3. After the simmering is finished, remove the top, add the coconut milk, and cook for another 4 minutes.
4. Pour the soup into a blender and pulse several times to purée it until it is creamy and smooth. Serve the soup right away in a big bowl.

Nutritional Info: Calories: 228 Fat: 19g Protein: 3g Carbs: 15g

Garlicky Broccoli with Cashew Soup

Preparation Time: 10 minutes
Cooking time: 25 minutes
Servings: 6

Ingredients:

- 5 cups plus 2 tablespoons water, divided
- 1 onion, finely chopped

- 4 garlic cloves, finely chopped
- 4 broccoli heads with stalks, heads cut into florets and stalks roughly chopped
- 1½ teaspoons sea salt, plus additional as needed
- 1 cup cashews, soaked in water for at least 4 hours, drained

Directions:

1. In a large pot, add 2 tablespoons of water, the onion, and the garlic. Sauté for 5 minutes, or until the onion is translucent.
2. Add the remaining water, salt, and broccoli. After bringing the mixture to a boil, turn down the heat. For 20 minutes, simmer with a cover on.
3. Pour the soup and cashews into a blender. until creamy and smooth, pulse to purée. Serve the soup right away after pouring it into a big bowl.

Nutritional Info: Calories: 224 Fat: 11g Protein: 11g Carbs: 26g

Squashy Carrot and Celery Soup

Preparation Time: 5 minutes
Cooking time: 30 minutes
Servings: 6
Ingredients:

- 4½ cups plus 2 tablespoons water, divided
- 1 onion, roughly chopped
- 1 large butternut squash, washed, peeled, ends trimmed, halved, seeded, and cut into ½-inch chunks
- 3 carrots, peeled and roughly chopped
- 2 celery stalks, roughly chopped

- 1 teaspoon sea salt, or to taste

Directions:

1. In a large saucepan, add 2 tablespoons of water, add the onion, and cook for 5 minutes, or until the onion is soft.
2. Include the remaining water, salt, butternut squash, carrots, and celery. up to a boil. Simmer for 25 minutes, or until the squash is tender, on low heat.
3. Add the soup to a food processor and pulse several times to purée it until it is creamy and smooth. Serve the soup right away after pouring it into a big bowl.

Nutritional Info: Calories: 104 Fat: 0g Protein: 2g Carbs: 27g

Mixed Greens Soup with Coconut Milk

Preparation Time: 10 minutes
Cooking time: 15 minutes
Servings: 4-6

Ingredients:

- 2 cups unsweetened coconut milk
- 3 cups water
- 1½ teaspoons sea salt, or to taste
- 1 bunch fresh parsley, rinsed, stemmed and roughly chopped
- 4 cups tightly packed kale, rinsed, stemmed, and roughly chopped
- 4 cups tightly packed spinach, rinsed, stemmed and roughly chopped

- 4 cups tightly packed collard greens, rinsed, stemmed and roughly chopped

Directions:

1. Add salt to the big pot after adding the coconut milk and water. Bring to a boil over high heat. Set the thermostat to a low setting.
2. Place one cup of each type of green in the pot and cook for five minutes, or until wilted. Continue by using the remaining greens. Simmer for 10 minutes, or until all the greens have wilted.
3. Pour the soup into a blender, and then blend it until it is smooth and creamy. Serve the soup right away after pouring it into a big bowl.

Nutritional Info: Calories: 334 Fat: 29g Protein: 7g Carbs: 18g

Onion Chipotle Soup with Sage

Preparation Time: 10 minutes
Cooking time: 11 minutes
Servings: 4
Ingredients:

- 2 tablespoons extra-virgin olive oil
- 1 onion, chopped
- 2 garlic cloves, cut into 1/8-inch-thick slices
- 1 (15-ounce / 425-g) can pumpkin purée
- 4 cups low-sodium vegetable broth
- 2 teaspoons chipotle powder
- 1 teaspoon sea salt
- ½ teaspoon freshly ground black pepper
- 2 tablespoons coconut oil
- 12 sage leaves, stemmed

Directions:

1. In a large saucepan, heat the olive oil over high heat until it shimmers. Sauté for 5 minutes, or until the onion becomes brown, after adding the onion and garlic.
2. Add the chipotle powder, salt, and freshly ground black pepper after adding the pumpkin purée and vegetable broth. Stir well to combine.

Bring the water to a boil. For five minutes, simmer over low heat. Coconut oil should be heated in a nonstick pan while doing this.

4. Stir in the sage leaves and heat for one minute, or until crispy.
5. After the soup has finished simmering, divide it into four bowls for serving. Add three sage leaves to each bowl as a garnish, then plate the food.

Nutritional Info: Calories: 380 Fat: 20g Protein: 10g Carbs: 45g

Pears with Peppered Fennel Soup

Preparation Time: 10 minutes
Cooking time: 13 minutes
Servings: 4-6
Ingredients:

- 2 tablespoons extra-virgin olive oil
- 1 fennel bulb, cut into ¼-inch-thick slices
- 2 leeks, white part only, sliced
- 2 pears, peeled, cored, and cut into ½-inch cubes
- 1 teaspoon sea salt
- ¼ teaspoon freshly ground black pepper
- ½ cup cashews
- 3 cups low-sodium vegetable broth
- 2 cups packed spinach

Directions:

1. In a large saucepan, heat the olive oil over high heat until it shimmers. Saute the fennel and leeks for 5 minutes, or until they are soft.
2. Include the pears and add salt and pepper to taste. additional three minutes of sautéing.
3. Include the veggie broth and cashews. up to a boil. Set the thermostat to a low setting. Five minutes of simmering under cover
4. Pour the soup and spinach into a blender. until creamy and smooth, pulse. Place the soup in a big serving dish and start serving right away.

Nutritional Info: Calories: 266 Fat: 15g Protein: 5g Carbs: 33g

Scallion with Minty Cucumber Salad

Preparation Time: 15 minutes
Cooking time: 0 minutes
Servings: 4
Ingredients:

- 1 bunch radishes, sliced thin
- 1 English cucumber, peeled and diced
- 2 cups packed spinach
- 3 large tomatoes, diced
- 1 tablespoon chopped fresh mint
- 1 tablespoon chopped fresh parsley
- 2 scallions, sliced
- 2 garlic cloves, minced
- 1 cup unsweetened plain almond yogurt
- 1 tablespoon apple cider vinegar
- 3 tablespoons freshly squeezed lemon juice

- 1 tablespoon sumac
- 2 tablespoons extra-virgin olive oil
- 1 teaspoon sea salt
- ¼ teaspoon freshly ground black pepper

Directions:

1. In a large salad bowl, combine all the ingredients. After thoroughly mixing, serve right away.

Nutritional Info: Calories: 195 Fat: 14g Protein: 4g Carbs: 15g

SAVORY RECIPES

Beef & Sweet Potato Enchilada Casserole

Preparation Time: 20 minutes
Cooking time: 20 minutes
Servings: 10
Ingredients:

- 2 sweet potatoes
- 1 pound ground beef
- 1 can black beans, drained
- 1 cup frozen corn
- 1 can red enchilada sauce
- 4 tablespoon chopped fresh cilantro
- 2 teaspoon ground cumin
- 1 teaspoon garlic powder
- 1 teaspoon onion powder
- 12 corn tortillas
- 1 small can diced olives
- 4 tablespoons coconut cream

Directions:

1. After cooking the sweet potatoes and peeling them, mash them with two teaspoons of cilantro. After thoroughly combining the beans, corn, sauce, and seasonings, cook the ground beef.
2. In a 9x13-inch pan, layer half of the meat mixture, half of the corn tortilla, and half of the coconut cream; repeat the layers.
3. Add sweet potatoes, olives, and cilantro as garnishes. Bake at

350°F for about 25 minutes, or until the cheese is melted. Cover with the remaining cream.

Nutritional Info: Calories: 315 Fat: 8.2 g Carbs: 5.4 g Protein: 31.6 g

Delicious Buckwheat with Mushrooms & Green Onions

Preparation Time: 20 minutes
Cooking time: 35 minutes
Servings: 6
Ingredients:

- 1 cup uncooked buckwheat
- 2 cup water
- 2 cups mushrooms
- 1 red onion, chopped
- 1 cup chopped green onions
- 3 tablespoons butter
- A pinch of salt and pepper

Directions:

1. In a saucepan, combine the buckwheat, salt, and water. Bring to a boil, then simmer for 25 minutes, or until the liquid is absorbed.
2. In a skillet, melt the butter and cook the red onion until it softens. Stir in the mushrooms and cook for about 5 minutes, or until they are golden brown.
3. Add the cooked buckwheat and turn off the heat. Add freshly chopped green onions on top before serving.

Nutritional Info: Calories: 166 Fat: 6.8 g Carbs: 20.1 g Protein: 5.1 g

Yummy Chicken and Sweet Potato Stew

Preparation Time: 15 minutes
Cooking time: 4-8 hours
Servings: 4-6
Ingredients:

- 1-pound boneless chicken breasts, with skin removed and cut into chunks
- 1 Vidalia onion, chopped
- 4 cloves garlic, crushed
- 3 carrots, peeled and diced
- 1 sweet potato, peeled and cut into cubes
- 2 cups chicken broth, preferably homemade
- 3 tablespoons balsamic vinegar
- 2-4 tablespoons tomato paste
- 2 teaspoons whole grain mustard
- 2 cups fresh baby spinach
- Freshly ground pepper and salt to taste

Directions:

1. In your slow cooker, combine all the ingredients and stir well to combine. Cook covered for 6 to 8 hours on low or 4-5 hours on high.
2. Add the baby spinach with just a few minutes remaining in the cooking process. Serve warm

Nutritional Info: Calories: 139 Fat: 3.7g Carbs: 2.6 g Protein: 5.4 g

Healthy Fried Brown Rice with Peas & Prawns

Preparation Time: 10 minutes
Cooking time: 10 minutes
Servings: 8

Ingredients:

- 1/2 cup frozen pea
- 2 cups cooked brown rice
- 2 teaspoons extra-virgin olive oil
- 1 red chilli, sliced
- 2 garlic cloves, sliced
- 1 red onion, sliced
- 1 cup large peeled prawn
- 1 bunch coriander, chopped
- 1 tablespoon fish sauce
- 1 tablespoon dark soy sauce
- 4 large eggs
- 1 tablespoon chilli sauce

Directions:

1. In a hot skillet, sauté the garlic, onion, and chili for about 3 minutes, or until golden. Stir in the prawns for about 1 minute, and then stir in the rice and peas

2. Cook until fully heated. Cook for a minute after stirring in the fish sauce, soy sauce, and coriander. Keep warm after removing yourself from the heat. Fry the eggs in hot oil while seasoning the pan.

3. Distribute the rice mixture among the four serving dishes, then place a fried egg on each one. Serve with coriander-topped chili sauce.

Nutritional Info: Calories: 278 Fat: 4.3 g Carbs: 44.9 g Protein: 8.3 g

Asparagus Quinoa & Steak Bowl

Preparation Time: 10 minutes
Cooking time: 15 minutes
Servings: 4
Ingredients:

- 1-1/2 cups white quinoa
- Olive oil cooking spray
- 3/4-pound lean steak, diced
- 1/2 tsp. low-sodium steak seasoning
- 1/2 cup chopped red bell pepper
- 1/2 cup chopped red onion
- 1 cup frozen asparagus cuts
- 2 ½ tbsp. soy sauce

Directions:

1. To cook quinoa, follow the directions on the box. Spray a big pan with cooking spray and preheat it to medium-high heat in the meantime.
2. After cooking the beef in the skillet for about 3 minutes, add the bell pepper and red onion and cook for an additional 3 minutes, or until the beef is browned.
Asparagus is added and cooked for a further 4 minutes, or until heated through. Before serving, combine the quinoa with the beef mixture by thoroughly stirring in the soy sauce.

Nutritional Info: Calories: 325 Fat: 8.2 g Carbs : 17.4 g Protein: 26.3 g

Seared Lemon Steak with Vegetables Stir-Fry

Preparation Time: 15 minutes
Cooking time: 10 minutes
Servings: 3-4
Ingredients:

- 1-pound lean steak
- ¼ cup fresh lemon juice
- 1 tablespoon lemon zest
- 1 ½ cups almond milk
- 2 teaspoons coconut oil
- 1 cup chopped red onion
- 4 cloves garlic, minced
- 2 cups shiitake mushrooms, diced
- 3 medium zucchinis
- 1 green pepper bell
- 1 red pepper bell
- 3 tomatoes
- 1 teaspoon curry powder
- 1 tablespoon ginger
- ¼ teaspoon salt
- ¼ teaspoon pepper

Directions:

1. Heat half the coconut oil in a pan over medium heat. Sear the meat for approximately 6 minutes on each side, or until cooked through and golden brown on the exterior. Rub the meat with lemon juice, salt, lemon zest, and cayenne pepper.
2. Wrap the meat in foil to keep it warm. Slice beans, tomatoes, bell peppers, zucchini, and bell peppers into bite-sized pieces.

3. In a skillet with hot oil, cook the red onion and garlic for 3 minutes before adding the mushrooms, zucchini, and bell peppers.

4. Add the tomatoes and almond milk, and simmer for a few minutes. Ginger, curry powder, salt, and pepper are used to season. Serve with steak slices on top.

Nutritional Info: Calories: 406 Fat: 33.6 g Carbs: 20.2 g Protein: 15.1 g

Vegetable Tabbouleh

Preparation Time: 5 minutes
Cooking time: 10 minutes
Servings: 2
Ingredients:

- 1 cup broccoli florets
- 1 chopped carrots
- 1 cup shredded cabbage
- 1 teaspoon sesame seeds
- A pinch of salt and pepper
- 1 cup cooked quinoa
- 1 cucumber, sliced
- ¼ cup fresh lemon juice
- Handful cilantro

Directions:

1. Stir-fry red onions, garlic, broccoli florets, chopped fresh chili, chopped carrots, shredded cabbage, and sesame seeds in hot but non-smoking oil in a skillet over medium heat.
2. Cook the vegetables for approximately 5 minutes, or until they are crisp and tender. Add salt and pepper, then turn off the heat.

3. To make a tasty and nutritious meal, top cooked quinoa with chopped cucumber, fresh cilantro, and a squeeze of lemon.

Nutritional Info: Calories: 447 Carbs: 48g Fat: 27g Protein: 9g

Peppered Steak with Cherry Tomatoes

Preparation Time: 10 minutes
Cooking time: 10 minutes
Servings: 4
Ingredients:

- 4 (250g) lean beef steaks
- 1 tablespoon extra-virgin olive oil
- 2 tablespoons pepper
- 1 bunch rocket
- 2 cups cherry tomatoes
- 4 cups green salad
- olive oil cooking spray

Directions:

1. Oil the steak with a brush. The steaks should be well covered in the pepper, which has been placed on a big platter.
2. After preheating the grill to medium-high, cook the steaks for approximately 5 minutes on each side, or until they are well-done. Cooked steaks should be transferred to a dish and kept warm.
3. Grill the tomatoes for approximately 5 minutes, turning them regularly, until they are soft. In the meantime,

Nutritional Info: Calories: 237 Fat: 11.1g Carbs: 10.7g Protein: 14.8g

Grilled Chicken Breast with Non-Fat Yogurt

Preparation Time: 2 hours
Cooking time: 10 minutes
Servings: 3
Ingredients:
For the Grilled Chicken:

- 3 boneless chicken breast halves, skinned
- 1 clove garlic, minced
- 1 tablespoon lemon juice, freshly squeezed
- 1 teaspoon extra virgin olive oil
- 1 teaspoon dried oregano
- Salt and freshly ground black pepper, to taste

For the yogurt:

- 1 cup nonfat Greek yogurt
- 1 clove garlic, minced
- 1 tsp. fresh dill, minced
- ½ cup cucumber, very thinly sliced or shredded

Directions:
1. Gently cut through the thickest portion of the chicken breast with a sharp knife, going all the way through, to allow you to open it up like a book. Repeat for the additional two halves.
2. In a big basin, combine the remaining chicken ingredients and marinate the chicken. Refrigerate for one and a half to two hours while covered with cling wrap. Heat your grill to a moderately hot setting.
3. Remove the marinated chicken from the liquid. Place the breasts on the grill rack after lightly greasing it.

4. Cook for 3 minutes on each side, or until desired doneness is achieved. In the meanwhile, put everything for the yogurt in a medium dish.

5. Place each breast on a sizable plate before serving. A dollop of the nutty yogurt should be placed on the side. Enjoy!

Nutritional Info: Calories: 318 Fat: 33. G Carbs: 8 g Protein: 37.2g

Delicious Low Fat Chicken Curry

Preparation Time: 10 minutes
Cooking time: 20 minutes
Servings: 1
Ingredients:

- 100 grams chicken, diced
- ¼ cup chicken broth
- Pinch of turmeric
- Dash of onion powder
- 1 tablespoon minced red onion
- Pinch of garlic powder
- ¼ teaspoon curry powder
- Pinch of sea salt
- Pinch of pepper
- Stevia, optional
- Pinch of cayenne

Directions:

1. In a small saucepan, combine the spices, chicken broth, and stevia; mix to combine. Add the chicken, garlic, onion, and pepper; heat until the chicken is fully cooked and the liquid has been reduced by half. Serve hot.

Nutritional Info: Calories: 170 Fat: 3.5 g Carbs: 2.3 g Protein: 30.5 g

Tilapia with Mushroom Sauce

Preparation Time: 15 minutes
Cooking time: 25 minutes
Servings: 4
Ingredients:

- 4 ounces tilapia fillets
- 2 teaspoon arrow root
- 1 cup mushrooms, sliced
- 1 clove garlic, finely chopped
- 1 small onion, thinly sliced
- 1 teaspoon extra-virgin olive oil
- ½ cup fresh parsley, roughly chopped
- 1 teaspoon thyme leaves, finely chopped
- ½ cup water
- A pinch of freshly ground black pepper
- A pinch of sea salt

Directions:

1. Set your oven to 350 degrees Fahrenheit. Over medium heat, add extra virgin olive oil to a frying pan; add onion, garlic, and mushrooms; sauté for about 4 minutes, or until mushrooms are just beginning to soften.
2. After about a minute, add the arrowroot, sea salt, thyme, and pepper. Cook for an additional minute while stirring in the parsley after the water has thickened.
3. Arrange the fish fillets on a baking sheet lined with parchment

paper, top with mushroom sauce, and bake for 20 minutes, or until the fish is thoroughly cooked.
Nutritional Info: Calories: 177 Fat: 3.7 g Carbs: 3.3 g Protein: 14.9 g

Ginger Chicken with Veggies

Preparation Time: 10 minutes
Cooking time: 5 minutes
Servings: 4
Ingredients:

- 2 cup skinless, boneless, and cooked chicken breast meat, diced
- 1 teaspoon extra virgin olive
- 1 teaspoon powdered ginger
- 2 red onions, sliced
- 4 cloves garlic, minced
- 1 bell pepper, sliced
- 1 cup thinly sliced carrots
- 1 cup finely chopped celery
- 1 cup chicken broth (not salted)

Directions:

1. In a medium-sized skillet, add the oil and cook the onion and garlic until they are translucent. When the vegetables are ready, add the remaining ingredients and simmer for a short while.

Nutritional Info: Calories: 425 Fat: 21.1g Carbs: 6.5 g Protein: 52g

Hot Lemon Prawns

Preparation Time: 15 minutes
Cooking time: 12 minutes
Servings: 4
Ingredients:

- 400g raw king prawns
- 1 teaspoon coconut oil
- 40g ginger, grated
- 2-4 green chillies, halved
- 4 curry leaves
- 1 onion, sliced
- 4 teaspoons lemon juice
- 3-4 teaspoons red chilli powder
- 2 teaspoons turmeric
- 1 teaspoon black pepper
- 40g grated coconut
- ½ small bunch coriander

Directions:

1. After rinsing and drying the prawns with a kitchen towel, place them in a large bowl and stir in the chili powder, turmeric, ginger, and lemon juice. Set the bowl aside.
2. In a saucepan over medium heat, add the onion, ginger, chilli, and curry leaves. Sauté for about 10 minutes, or until the onion is translucent. Add the prawns to the marinade after adding the black pepper and stirring.
3. Cook for about 2 minutes, or until fully done. Add seasoning and more lemon juice drizzle. Coriander and grated coconut should be added to the serving of prawns. Enjoy!

Nutritional Info: Calories: 171 Fat: 8 g Carbs: 4 g Protein: 19 g

Delicious Chicken Tikka Skewers

Preparation Time: 20 minutes
Cooking time: 20 minutes
Servings: 4

Ingredients:

- 4 boneless, skinless chicken breasts, diced
- 2 tablespoons hot curry paste
- 1 red onion, sliced
- ½ cucumber, sliced
- For the cucumber salad
- 250g pack cherry tomatoes
- 50g pack lamb's lettuce
- juice 1 lemon
- 150g nonfat Greek yogurt
- handful chopped coriander leaves

Directions:

1. Soak skewers in water in a dish.
2. Combine curry paste and yogurt in a dish, add chicken, and then marinate for an hour.
3. In the meantime, combine fresh lemon juice, red onion, cucumber, and coriander in a bowl. Refrigerate until ready to serve.
4. Thread chicken and cherry tomatoes onto skewers, then grill for 20 minutes, or until the chicken is cooked through and the exterior is well browned.
5. Divide the salad among serving dishes and top with two chicken skewers. Add the lettuce and mix thoroughly. Enjoy!

Nutritional Info: Calories: 234 Fat: 4 g Carbs: 9.7 g Protein: 40 g

Grilled Chicken with Salad Wrap

Preparation Time: 5 minutes
Cooking time: 0 minutes
Servings: 2
Ingredients:

- 2 lettuce leaves
- ½ coddled egg
- 1 cup diced cherry tomatoes
- 6 cups chopped curly kale
- 8 ounces sliced grilled chicken
- 1 clove garlic, minced
- 1/2 teaspoon Dijon mustard
- 1 teaspoon raw honey
- 1 teaspoon olive oil
- 1/8 cup fresh lemon juice
- Salt & pepper

Directions:

1. In a large bowl, combine half the egg, honey, mustard, minced garlic, extra virgin olive oil, fresh lemon juice, salt, and pepper.
2. Spread the mixture onto lettuce leaves, top with chicken, kale, and cherry tomatoes, and roll up to make wraps. Serve immediately after cutting in half!

Nutritional Info: Calories: 386 Fat: 2.6 g Carbs: 28.5 g Protein: 32.5 g

MEAT RECIPES

Pork Egg Roll Soup

Preparation Time: 10 minutes
Cooking time: 2 hours
Servings: 4
Ingredients:

- Avocado oil (1 tbsp.)
- Ribbed pork (1 lb.)
- 2 medium onion (chopped)
- Meat broth (5 ½ cups)
- Cabbage (1 ½ lb., chopped)
- Carrot (1lb. shredded)
- Garlic (1 clove, chopped)
- Salt (1 tsp.)
- ginger (1 1/2 tsp, ground)
- Coconut sauce (3/4 cup)
- Cornstarch (3 tbsp.)

Directions:

1. Add the oil to the stock pot and heat it up over medium heat. Once it's heated, add your meat and brown it well.
2. Include your coconut sauce, onions, cabbage, stock, garlic, salt, and ginger. Cook on low heat for one and a half hours.
3. Add 3 tablespoons of cornstarch to 2/3 cup of broth in a small bowl, stir into the soup, and let simmer for an additional 30 minutes (at a low temperature). Serve.

Nutritional Info: Calories 218 Fat 12.9g Protein 18.7g Carbs 7.6g

Pork Casserole

Preparation Time: 15 minutes
Cooking time: 1 hour & 40 minutes
Servings: 4
Ingredients:

- 2 tbsp olive oil
- 1 lb pork, cut into cubes
- 3 onions, quarter cut
- 1 yellow pepper, cut into thick strips
- 4 red peppers, quarter cut
- 1 lb ripe tomatoes, quarter cut
- 5 tbsp sun-dried tomato paste
- 6 oz green olives
- 1 can (2 oz) black olives
- 2 ½ cups water
- 1 cup red wine
- 6 tbsp fresh oregano, chopped

Directions:
1. Turn a pot's heat to medium. Olive oil should be added to the saucepan. Pork is browned for five minutes.
2. Include the red, yellow, and onion peppers. Cook for three minutes. Other than the fresh oregano, add the other ingredients.
3. Shield the pan. 1 hour and 40 minutes of cooking time Before serving, garnish with fresh oregano.
Nutritional Info: Calories 400 Fat 10.5g Protein 28.5g Carbs 22.5g

Delicious Pork Roast Baracoa

Preparation Time: 10 minutes
Cooking time: 8 hours
Servings:
Ingredients:

- 7 pounds of pork roast, cut into chunks
- 1 can diced green chilies
- 6 cloves minced garlic
- 1 tbsp cumin
- 8 tsp salt
- Juice from 3 different limes
- 1 diced onion
- 2-3 chopped chipotles in adobo sauce
- 9 tbsp apple cider vinegar
- 1 tbsp coriander
- 1 tsp black pepper
- ½ cup of fat free pork broth of choice

Directions:

1. Combine all of your ingredients before adding them to the slow cooker. Cook on low for 6 to 8 hours, or until the meat is tender enough to shred.
2. Dice the meat, then combine it with the liquids. For optimal results, use a fork while serving.

Nutritional Info: Calories 283 Fat 11.7g Protein 37.1g Carbs 8g

Swedish Meatballs & Mushrooms Gravy

Preparation Time: 15 minutes
Cooking time: 40 minutes
Servings: 6-8

Ingredients:

- 1 onion (large), chopped
- 1 pound/ 450 grams ground pork
- 1 pound/450 grams ground pork
- 1 teaspoon sage (dried)
- ½ cup coconut milk, bone broth, or water
- ½ teaspoon mace (ground)
- ½ teaspoon sea salt
- ¼ cup parsley (fresh), minced, divided
- 10 cups (cremini/button) mushrooms, sliced
- 11 tablespoons onion (dried), chopped
- 12 tablespoons coconut aminos

Directions:

1. Combine the salt, mace, dried onion, pork, and 3 tablespoons parsley in a bowl. Make 1-inch meatballs out of the mixture.
2. Fill your IP with the mushrooms, fresh onion, coconut milk, broth, and water, along with the coconut aminos. the meatballs, please.
3. Close the pressure valve and lock the lid. Meat or stew is set for 35 minutes. Open the lid and press QPR when the timer sounds.
4. Using a slotted spoon, carefully transfer the meatballs to a serving plate. Puree what's left in the saucepan using a stick blender or a powerful blender.
5. To thin, add coconut milk, broth, or water as required. Add the remaining parsley as a garnish after pouring the sauce over the meatballs.

Nutritional Info: Calories 278 Fat 12.2g Protein 37g Carbs 4g

Cherry & Apple Pork

Preparation Time: 10 minutes
Cooking time: 35 minutes
Servings: 4
Ingredients:

- olive oil, 1 tbsp., extra virgin, plus some for squash
- 13 cups dice apple
- 2/3 cup pit cherry
- 1/3 cup diced onion
- 1/3 cup diced celery
- ½ cup apple juice, sugar free
- 1/8 teaspoon salt
- 1/8 teaspoon black pepper
- 1 1/3 pounds boneless pork loin

Directions:

1. Fill an Instant Pot with all the ingredients and secure the lid. 40 minutes of cooking time with the meat or stew option are required.
2. Perform a fast pressure release. Serve.

Nutritional Info: Calories 237 Fat 12g Protein 0.7g Carbs 6g

Paleo Italian Pork

Preparation Time: 5 minutes
Cooking time: 2 hours & 45 minutes
Servings: 4
Ingredients:

- 16 lbs. grass-fed pork roast, cut into pieces
- 1 tablespoons garlic powder
- 1 tsp onion powder

- 1 teaspoon ginger powder
- 1 teaspoon oregano
- 1 teaspoon basil
- 1 teaspoons salt
- 2 ½ cups chicken broth
- 14 tablespoons apple cider vinegar

Directions:

1. Combine salt, oregano, basil, ginger, garlic, and onion in a bowl. To completely integrate, stir.
2. Rub your roast with this mixture, then put it aside. Heat up a deep pot over medium-low. When it's heated, add your roast and let it cook evenly on both sides (about 2 minutes per side).
3. Pour apple cider vinegar and pork broth into the pan. Put a lid on the pot and set the timer for 2 hours and 45 minutes on low heat. Take the pork roast out of the pot. Your meat should be placed on a small platter.
4. With two forks, shred the meat. To do this, stab the first fork into the meat directly in the center while holding it steady.
5. After that, insert the second fork with its teeth facing you into the meat where the first one was and pull it toward you.
6. Keep doing this until all of the meat has been shred. Enjoy after serving.

Nutritional Info: Calories 288 Fat 11g Protein 42g Carbs 1.6g

Corned Pork

Preparation Time: 5 minutes
Cooking time: 2 hours & 30 minutes
Servings: 6
Ingredients:

- 3-pounds corned pork brisket
- 2 cups red potatoes, whole
- 2 onions, halved
- 9-10 garlic cloves
- 2½ cups of pork broth
- 1 cabbage, chopped
- 1 bay leaf
- 2 cloves
- 12-15 peppercorns
- 2 tablespoons coriander seeds
- ¼ teaspoon cumin seeds
- 2 cinnamon sticks
- 2 tablespoons cornstarch

Directions:

1. Add the pork, red potatoes, onion, all of the spices, and the garlic to a large saucepan. Covered.

2. Prepare for 2 hours and 20 minutes over medium heat. Once everything is ready, add the cabbage to the saucepan and boil it for a few minutes on high heat, or until it is tender.

3. After that, take the vegetables and pork from the saucepan but save the drippings.

4. Combine the cornstarch and drippings. Then, add this mixture to the pig juices and bring to a boil over medium heat. Cook for another 3–4 minutes at a reduced flame. Enjoy after serving.

Nutritional Info: Calories 379.2 Fat 10.6g Protein 59.1g Carbs 9.7g

Chipotle Pork Carnitas

Preparation Time: 15 minutes
Cooking time: 2 hours & 45 minutes

Servings: 8
Ingredients:

- pork shoulder, blade roast, 2 lb, boneless and trimmed
- ½ tsp garlic powder
- dry adobo seasoning, ¼ tsp
- 2 bay leaves
- 3 chipotle peppers
- 1 ¾ cup chicken stock
- Oregano, ¼ tsp, dried
- 4 tsp salt
- ½ tsp sazon
- 1 tsp cumin
- 5 garlic cloves, cut into slivers
- Black pepper to taste

Directions:
1. For 5 minutes on high heat, brown the pork in a large pan on all sides. Pork should be taken out of the pan and allowed to cool.
2. Insert garlic slivers all over your pork by inserting a knife about an inch into the meat. Garlic powder, adobo, oregano, sazon, and cumin are used to season the pork. Fill your pot with chicken stock.
3. Add the bay leaves and chipotle peppers after placing the pork in a large pot. Cook for two hours and forty minutes at a low temperature with the lid on.
4. Using forks, shred the pork, then mix it with the liquids. Remove the bay leaves, then thoroughly combine. Enjoy a hot serving.

Nutritional Info: Calories 172 Fat 4.1g Protein 30.2g Carbs 2g

Slow Cooked Pork Tenderloin

Preparation Time: 5 minutes
Cooking time: 8 hours
Servings: 6
Ingredients:

- 7 pounds of pork tenderloin
- ½ cup low sodium chicken broth
- 8 tbsp. stevia
- ½ tsp. garlic powder and cumin
- Salt and pepper for taste
- ¼ cup balsamic vinegar
- 9 tbsp. soy sauce
- ¼ tsp. chili powder

Directions:

1. Add the vinegar and soy sauce to the slow cooker and stir to combine.
2. Add the rest and drizzle part of the vinegar mixture over the meat. Cook the meat for 6 to 8 hours with the cover on, or until it is very soft.
3. You may lower the cooking liquid if you'd like to make a lovely glaze. Put it on the broiler for at least 4-5 minutes if you want the outside to be crispier.

Nutritional Info: Calories 264 Fat 6.4g Protein 40.6g Carbs 8.3g

Pork with Carrots & Apples

Preparation Time: 10 minutes
Cooking time: 10 minutes
Servings: 4
Ingredients:

- 14 ½ boneless skinless pork loins (about ½ inch thick or 15 ounces each)
- 1 tablespoon of extra virgin olive oil, divided
- 1 teaspoon ground ginger
- ½ teaspoon ground sage
- ¼ teaspoon freshly ground black pepper
- 1 tablespoon unsalted fat free butter
- 1 large apple (Pink Lady works well), peeled, cored and cubed
- 1 cup diced carrots (approximately 5 16 small)
- ¼ cup water

Directions:

1. Cover the pork with half the olive oil. Rub the pepper, sage, and ginger mixture on the pork chops' top and bottom surfaces.
2. In a big skillet over medium heat, heat the remaining half of the oil. Pork should be added to the pan and cooked for 3 to 4 minutes on each side until brown before being transferred to a dish.
3. Add carrots, apples, and fat-free butter to the pan and cook until the vegetables are golden brown.
4. Add about 14 cups more water and stir; simmer until the vegetables are soft. Cook the meat in the skillet until it is heated through.

Nutritional Info: Calories 337 Fat 6g Protein 33g Carbs 11g

Shredded Pork Tacos

Preparation Time: 10 minutes
Cooking time: 2 hours & 45 minutes
Servings: 11
Ingredients:

- 17 ½ lbs. pork shoulder roast (trimmed, boneless)
- 6 garlic cloves (sliced)
- 1 ½ teaspoons cumin
- ¼ teaspoon oregano (dry)
- 18 teaspoons salt
- 19 bay leaves
- ¼ teaspoon adobo seasoning (dry)
- ½ teaspoon garlic powder
- 20 chipotle peppers (placed in adobo sauce)
- ½ teaspoon sazon
- Black pepper, to taste
- 1¾ cups chicken broth (reduced-sodium)
- Romaine lettuce leaves (enough to serve)

Directions:

1. Season the pork with salt and pepper, then cook it for 5 minutes over medium heat in a saucepan.
2. Make cuts in the pork with a knife and insert pieces of garlic. Over the pork, sprinkle oregano, adobo spice, cumin, sazon, and garlic powder.
3. Add the other ingredients to the saucepan after adding the meat back in. Cook on low heat for 2 hours and 40 minutes, covered , or until thoroughly done.
4. Using forks, shred the pork, then add it back to the pot. Throw out the bay leaves. Warm Romaine lettuce leaves are served.

Nutritional Info: Calories 130 Fat 7g Protein 20g Carbs 1g

Pork Ragu with Tagliatelle

Preparation Time: 5 minutes
Cooking time: 50 minutes

Servings: 4
Ingredients:

- 9 oz. Tagliatelle
- 14 oz. extra lean minced pork
- 14 oz. tomatoes, chopped
- 21 garlic cloves, chopped
- 22 carrots, finely diced
- 23 celery sticks, chopped
- 1 finely chopped onion
- 24 tablespoons tomato puree
- 1 teaspoon olive oil
- ½ teaspoon dried oregano
- ½ teaspoon stevia
- 1 bay leaf
- 25 cups water
- Salt and pepper, to taste

Directions:

1. In a large nonstick frying pan, heat the oil. Add the minced pork and cook, breaking up the meat as it cooks, for 5 minutes.
2. Place the cooked meat in a large saucepan. In a separate frying pan, heat more olive oil. Add the carrots, onions, and celery. Cook over low heat for 10 minutes, adding a little water if necessary.
3. After another 2 minutes of cooking, stir in the garlic and oregano and pour the mixture into your saucepan. Combine water, bay leaf, and stevia.
4. Add salt and pepper, bring to a boil, then reduce the heat and simmer for 45 minutes, stirring occasionally, to create a rich, thick sauce.
5. Once the ragu is prepared, boil the pasta according to the

package directions and drain. Add sauce on top after dividing into bowls.

Nutritional Info: Calories 363 Fat 8.9g Protein 25.7g Carbs 8.9g

Pork with Olives & Feta

Preparation Time: 10 minutes
Cooking time: 60 minutes
Servings: 4
Ingredients:

- 26 lb. pork stew meat, cubed
- 30 oz spicy diced tomatoes with juice
- ½ cup black olives
- ½ cup green olives
- ½ tsp salt
- ¼ tsp black pepper
- 27 cups cooked rice

Directions:

1. Fill the Instant Pot with the pork, tomatoes, black olives, and green olives. Add salt and pepper to taste.
2. Cover the pot. Select Manual. One hour on high in the oven Add the feta cheese on top. Serve with rice if desired.

Nutritional Info: Calories 378 Fat 9g Protein 36g Carbs 14g

Bone in Ham with Maple-Honey Glaze

Preparation Time: 5 minutes
Cooking time: 1 hour & 15 minutes

Servings: 14
Ingredients:

- 8 tablespoons maple syrup
- 4 tablespoons honey
- 1½ cups orange juice
- 1 cup pineapple juice, sugar free
- 1 cinnamon sticks
- 1 bone-in ham

Directions:

1. In a saucepan over medium heat, combine the maple syrup, honey, orange, pineapple, and cinnamon to make a glaze. Mix thoroughly, then heat the mixture until it thickens.
2. Take the heat off and leave it aside. Put your ham in a deep pot, cover it, and simmer it for 50 minutes over medium heat.
3. Place the ham in an oven-safe dish and pour the glaze on top. Place the pan under the broiler for the caramelized glaze. Enjoy after serving.

Nutritional Info: Calories 60 Fat 1g Protein 10g Carbs 3g

FISH RECIPES

Scallop and Strawberry Salad

Preparation time: 2 hours
Cooking time: 6 minutes
Servings: 2
Ingredients:

- 4 ounces scallops
- ½ cup Pico de gallo
- ½ cup chopped strawberries
- 1 tablespoon lime juice
- Salt and black pepper to the taste

Directions:

1. Place the scallops in a heated pan over medium heat. Cook for 3 minutes on each side before transferring to a bowl.
2. Add salt, pepper, lime juice, pico de gallo, and strawberries. After two hours, toss and serve cold. Enjoy!

Nutritional Info: Calories 83 Fat 1g Carbs 5g Protein 14g

Halibut with Fruit Salad

Preparation time: 10 minutes
Cooking time: 10 minutes
Servings: 4
Ingredients:

- 4 halibut steaks, boneless
- 1 small cucumber, chopped
- 2 kiwis, peeled and chopped
- 3 cups strawberries, halved and then sliced
- 2 tablespoons olive oil
- Juice of ½ lemon
- A pinch of sea salt and black pepper
- A pinch of cayenne pepper
- ¼ teaspoon cinnamon powder
- 1/3 cup basil, chopped
- 6 cups micro greens

Directions:

1. Combine the cucumber with the kiwi, strawberries, lemon juice, salt, pepper, basil, and half the oil in a bowl.
2. Rub the halibut steaks thoroughly with the remaining oil after seasoning with salt, pepper, cinnamon, and cayenne.
3. Preheat a skillet over medium-high heat, add the fish steaks, and cook for 5 minutes on each side. Then, divide the fish among plates and serve with the fruit salad on the side. Enjoy!

Nutritional Info: Calories 270 Fat 6g Carbs 13g Protein 15g

Poached Cod and Leeks

Preparation time: 10 minutes
Cooking time: 20 minutes
Servings: 4
Ingredients:

- 4 cod fillets, skinless and boneless
- 2 cups veggie stock

- 2 tablespoons lemon juice
- 1 tablespoon fresh grated ginger
- 4 teaspoons lemon zest
- A pinch of sea salt and black pepper
- 3 leeks, chopped
- 2 tablespoons olive oil
- 1 pound kale, chopped
- ½ teaspoon sesame oil

Directions:

1. Combine the salt, pepper, and lemon zest in a bowl before stirring the mixture and applying it to the fish. Over medium heat, warm up a pan with the stock.

2. Stir in the leeks, ginger, and lemon juice before cooking for a few minutes at a simmer. Add fish fillets to this mixture, cover the pan, and poach the fish for 10 minutes. Then, remove the fish from the pan, drain the cooking liquid, and keep the leeks aside.

3. Add the kale to a skillet that has been heated with the olive oil and cook for 3 to 4 minutes. Cook for another five minutes after adding the strained soup.

4. Stir in the saved leeks, simmer for another two minutes, and then turn off the heat. Place each fillet of fish in a bowl, then top with the leek soup. Serve the sesame oil with a drizzle. Enjoy!

Nutritional Info: Calories 278 Fat 3g Carbs 14g Protein 15g

Cilantro Halibut with Coconut Milk

Preparation time: 10 minutes
Cooking time: 10 minutes
Servings: 4
Ingredients:

- ¼ cup coconut milk
- ¼ cup chopped cilantro
- 1 tablespoon green curry paste
- ¼ cup chopped basil
- 2 teaspoons coconut aminos
- ½ teaspoon ground turmeric
- 4 halibut fillets, boneless
- 1 tablespoon avocado oil
- 1 red chili pepper, chopped

Directions:

1. Puree the cilantro in your blender together with the coconut milk, curry paste, turmeric, chili pepper, and basil.
2. Add the halibut fillets to an oil-coated pan and fry over medium-high heat for 4 minutes on each side.
3. Gently toss the fish with the coconut mixture, cook for an additional 2 minutes, then divide the dish into plates and serve. Enjoy!

Nutritional Info: Calories 210 Fat 3g Carbs 12g Protein 16

Easy Baked Cod

Preparation time: 10 minutes
Cooking time: 12 minutes
Servings: 2
Ingredients:

- 2 cod fillets, boneless
- 1 garlic cloves, minced
- 1 teaspoon olive oil
- Black pepper to the taste

- 3 sun-dried tomatoes, chopped
- 1 small red onion, sliced
- ½ fennel bulb, thinly sliced
- 4 black olives, pitted and sliced
- 2 rosemary springs
- ¼ teaspoon red pepper flakes

Directions:

1. Add the cod, garlic, black pepper, tomatoes, onions, fennel, olives, rosemary, and pepper flakes to the oil-greased baking dish.
2. Place the fish and vegetables on plates, cover the dish, and bake it at 400 degrees F for 14 minutes. Then, remove the rosemary. Enjoy!

Nutritional Info: Calories 260 Fat 4g Carbs 10g Protein 16g

Herbed Salmon with Onions

Preparation time: 10 minutes
Cooking time: 30 minutes
Servings: 2

Ingredients:

- 16 ounces pearl onions
- A drizzle of olive oil
- 2 medium salmon fillets, boneless
- 1 tablespoon dried parsley
- 1 teaspoon dried rosemary
- Black pepper to the taste

Directions:

1. Place the salmon in a baking dish and season with black pepper, parsley, and rosemary. A little tossing, 30 minutes at 375 degrees F in the oven, dividing among plates, and serving Enjoy!

Nutritional Info: Calories 260 Fat 3g Carbs 7g Protein 16g

Chinese Salmon

Preparation time: 10 minutes
Cooking time: 10 minutes
Servings: 2
Ingredients:

- 2 salmon steaks
- 4 tablespoons chopped green onions
- 4 tablespoons coconut aminos
- 2 garlic cloves, minced
- 2 tablespoons olive oil
- 1 teaspoon saffron powder

Directions:

1. Combine the green onions, aminos, garlic, oil, and saffron in a bowl. Salmon steaks are added, thoroughly mixed, and then placed on a preheated grill over medium heat.
2. Grill for five minutes per side. Serve the mixture between plates along with a side salad. Enjoy!

Nutritional Info: Calories 251 Fat 8g Carbs 13g Protein 16g

Spinach and Scallop

Preparation time: 10 minutes
Cooking time: 10 minutes

Servings: 4
Ingredients:

- 12 jumbo sea scallops
- A pinch of sea salt and black pepper
- A drizzle of olive oil
- 6 garlic cloves, minced
- 1 cup chopped yellow onion
- 12 ounces baby spinach

Directions:

1. Place the oil-coated pan over medium heat, add the scallops, season with salt and pepper, and cook for 3 minutes on each side before dividing among plates.
2. Reheat the pan to medium heat, add the onions and garlic, stir, and cook for 3 minutes. Toss in the spinach, cook for an additional three minutes, and then serve with the scallops. Enjoy!

Nutritional Info: Calories 206 Fat 6g Carbs 7g Protein 17g

Crab Salad

Preparation time: 10 minutes
Cooking time: 0 minutes
Servings: 3
Ingredients:

- 2 cups avocado, peeled, pitted and cubed
- 1 cup chopped cucumber
- 2 cups canned crab, drained and flaked
- 2 teaspoons chopped parsley
- A pinch of salt and black pepper

- ½ tablespoon olive oil
- 1 tablespoon lime juice

Directions:

1. Combine the avocado with the crab, cucumber, parsley, salt, pepper, oil, and lime juice in a salad bowl. Stir thoroughly, then plate. Enjoy!

Nutritional Info: Calories 260 Fat 17g Carbs 11g Protein 18g

Garlic Cod Soup

Preparation time: 2 hours
Cooking time: 20 minutes
Servings: 4
Ingredients:

- 2 pounds cod fillets, cubed
- 10 garlic cloves, minced
- 3 tablespoons olive oil
- 1 tablespoon lemon juice
- ¼ cup chopped parsley
- 1 yellow onion, chopped
- 2 tomatoes, chopped
- 1 tablespoon tomato paste
- 2 ½ cups veggie stock
- A pinch of sea salt and black pepper
- 10 cherry tomatoes, halved

Directions:

1. Combine the fish, 6 garlic cloves, 2 tablespoons oil, parsley, and lemon juice in a bowl. After coating the fish, cover the bowl and

place it in the refrigerator for two hours to marinade.

2. Add the onion to a pot with the remaining oil, stir, and cook for 2 minutes over medium-high heat.

3. Mix in the remaining garlic, tomatoes, tomato paste, stock, salt, and pepper along with the fish that has been marinated. Cook for 10 minutes after bringing it to a simmer.

4. Stir in the cherry tomatoes, cook the soup for an additional 6 minutes, and then serve the soup in bowls. Enjoy!

Nutritional Info: Calories 160 Fat 2g Carbs 4g Protein 7g

Chili Coconut Salmon

Preparation time: 10 minutes
Cooking time: 15 minutes
Servings: 6
Ingredients:

- 1 ¼ cups shredded coconut, unsweetened
- 1 pound salmon, cubed
- 1/3 cup coconut flour
- A pinch of salt and black pepper
- 1 egg
- 2 tablespoons olive oil
- ¼ cup water
- 4 red chilies, chopped
- 3 garlic cloves, minced
- ¼ cup balsamic vinegar
- ½ cup raw honey

Directions:

1. Stir together the coconut flour and a little bit of salt in a bowl. Put the shredded coconut in a third dish, and whisk the egg with black pepper in a separate basin.
2. Toss the salmon cubes with the shredded coconut mixture before dipping them in the egg and coconut flour mixture. Salmon should be added to a hot skillet with oil and cooked for 3 minutes on each side before being divided among plates.
3. Bring the water in a skillet to a medium-high heat and add the chiles, cloves, vinegar, and honey. Stir, gently boil for four minutes, then simmer for another two. After that, sprinkle over the salmon and serve. Enjoy!

Nutritional Info: Calories 211 Fat 5g Carbs 11g Protein 15

Clams with Olives Mix

Preparation time: 10 minutes
Cooking time: 10 minutes
Servings: 2
Ingredients:

- 3 tablespoons olive oil
- 2-pound little clams, scrubbed
- ½ teaspoon dried thyme
- 1 shallot, minced
- ½ cup veggie stock
- 2 garlic cloves, minced
- 1 apple, cored and chopped
- Juice of ½ lemon

Directions:

1. Place a pan with the oil over medium-high heat, add the shallots, and stir for 3–4 minutes.
2. Include the stock, clams, apple, lemon juice, and thyme. 6 minutes later, stir again, divide into bowls, and serve. Enjoy!

Nutritional Info: Calories 180 Fat 9g Carbs 8g Protein 10g

SOUPS & STEW

Classy Soup with Carrot and Ginger

Preparation Time: 10 minutes
Cooking time: 30 minutes
Servings: 6-8
Ingredients:

- 1 large onion, peeled and roughly chopped
- 4½ cups plus 2 tablespoons water, divided
- 8 carrots, peeled and roughly chopped
- 1½-inch piece thin fresh ginger, sliced
- 1¼ teaspoons sea salt
- 2 cups coconut milk, unsweetened

Directions:

1. In a big pot over medium heat, sauté the onion in 2 tablespoons of water for about 5 minutes, or until soft.
2. Include the salt, ginger, remaining 4 1 2 cups of water, and carrots. up to a boil. Low heat should be used to cover the pot. For 20 minutes, simmer.
3. Add the coconut milk and heat for 4 to 5 minutes. Working in batches if necessary and being careful with the hot liquid, blend the soup in a blender until creamy.

Nutritional Info: Calories: 228 Fat: 19g Carbs: 15g Protein: 3g

Creamy Soup with Broccoli

Preparation Time: 12 minutes

Cooking time: 25 minutes
Servings: 6
Ingredients:

- 1 onion, finely chopped
- 4 garlic cloves, finely chopped
- 5 cups plus 2 tablespoons water, divided
- 1½ teaspoons sea salt, plus additional as needed
- 4 broccoli heads with stalks, heads cut into florets, and stalks roughly chopped
- 1 cup cashews, soaked in water for 4 hours

Directions:

1. In a big pot over medium heat, cook the onion and garlic in 2 tablespoons of water for about 5 minutes, or until soft.
2. Add the broccoli, salt, and remaining 5 cups of water. up to a boil. Low heat and a cover are required. For 20 minutes, simmer.
3. The cashews are drained and cleaned. Put them in a blender.
4. Fill the blender with the soup. Working in batches if necessary and being careful around the hot liquid, blend until the mixture is smooth. If necessary, taste and adjust the seasoning.

Nutritional Info: Calories: 224 Fat: 11g Carbs: 26g Protein: 11g

Classic Soup with Butternut Squash

Preparation Time: 20 minutes
Cooking time: 30 minutes
Servings: 6
Ingredients:

- 1 onion, chopped roughly

- 4½ cups plus 2 tablespoons water, divided
- 1 large butternut squash, washed, peeled, ends trimmed, halved, seeded, and cut into ½-inch chunks
- 2 celery stalks, chopped roughly
- 3 carrots, peeled and chopped roughly
- 1 teaspoon sea salt, plus additional as needed

Directions:

1. In a big pot over medium heat, cook the onion for about 5 minutes, or until soft, in 2 tablespoons of water.
2. Include the salt, carrot, celery, and squash. up to a boil. low-temperature setting For 25 minutes, simmer with a cover on.
3. Blend the soup until it is smooth, if necessary, working in batches and being careful around the hot liquid. If required, taste and adjust the seasoning.

Nutritional Info: Calories: 104 Carbs: 27g Fat: 0g Protein: 2g

Thai Soup with Potato

Preparation Time: 10 minutes
Cooking time: 20-25 minutes
Servings: 4-6
Ingredients:

- 3 large sweet potatoes, cubed
- 2 cups water
- One 14 ounces can coconut milk
- ½-inch piece fresh ginger, sliced
- ½ cup almond butter
- Zest of 1 lime
- Juice of 1 lime

- 1 teaspoon salt, plus additional as needed

Directions:

1. In a large pot over high heat, combine the sweet potatoes, water, coconut milk, and ginger. up to a boil. Cover the pan and lower the heat.
2. Simmer the potatoes for 20 to 25 minutes, or until they are fork-tender. Add the potatoes, ginger, and cooking liquid to a blender.
3. Include the salt, lime juice, zest, and almond butter. Until smooth, blend. If necessary, taste and adjust the seasoning.

Nutritional Info: Calories: 653 Fat: 42g Carbs: 64g Protein: 12g

Extraordinary Creamy Green Soup

Preparation Time: 10 minutes
Cooking time: 15 minutes
Servings: 4-6

Ingredients:

- 3 cups water
- 2 cups coconut milk, unsweetened
- 1½ teaspoons sea salt, plus additional as needed
- 4 cups tightly packed kale, washed thoroughly, stemmed, and roughly chopped
- 4 cups tightly packed spinach, stemmed and roughly chopped
- 4 cups tightly packed collard greens, stemmed and roughly chopped
- 1 bunch fresh parsley, stemmed and roughly chopped

Directions:

1. In a large pot over high heat, bring the water, coconut milk, and salt to a boil. Set the thermostat to a low setting.
2. After adding the first cup, wait for the kale, spinach, and collard greens to wilt before adding the second cup. Continue until the whole pot of greens has been added.
3. Simmer for 8 to 10 minutes. Working in batches if necessary and taking care of the hot liquid, blend the soup until it is smooth. Before serving, taste and adjust the seasoning.

Nutritional Info: Calories: 334 Fat: 29g Carbs: 18g Protein: 7g

Zingy Soup with Ginger, Carrot, and Lime

Preparation Time: 5 minutes
Cooking time: 40 minutes
Servings: 2

Ingredients:

- 2 tablespoon olive oil
- 1 teaspoon mustard seeds, ground
- 1 teaspoon coriander seeds, ground
- 1 teaspoon curry powder
- 1 teaspoon ginger, minced
- 4 cups carrots, thinly sliced
- 2 cups onions, chopped
- zest and juice of 1 lime
- 4 cups low-salt vegetable broth
- black pepper

Directions:

1. In a pan over medium heat, add the seeds and curry powder and cook for 1 minute. Cook for another minute after adding the ginger.
2. After that, add the carrots, onions, and lime zest and cook for a

minimum of two minutes, or until the vegetables are soft.

3. Add the broth, bring to a boil, then reduce the heat slightly and simmer for 30 minutes.

4. Permit cooling. In a food processor, puree the mixture until it is smooth. Serve with black pepper and lime juice.

Nutritional Info: Calories: 919 Fat: 51g Carbs: 105g Protein: 13g

Native Asian Soup with Squash and Shitake

Preparation Time: 10 minutes
Cooking time: 45 minutes
Servings: 2
Ingredients:

- 15 dried shiitake mushrooms, soaked in water
- 6 cups low salt vegetable stock
- ½ butternut squash, peeled and cubed
- 1 tablespoon sesame oil
- 1 onion, quartered and sliced into rings
- 1 large garlic clove, chopped
- 4 stems of pak choy or equivalent
- 1 sprig of thyme or 1 tablespoon dried thyme
- 1 teaspoon tabasco sauce

Directions:

1. Before sweating the onions and garlic, heat the sesame oil in a big pan over medium-high heat. Before adding the squash, add the vegetable stock and bring to a boil over high heat.

2. Reduce the heat, cover, and simmer for 25–30 minutes. If not already done, soak the mushrooms in water, press out the liquid, and then add it to the stock in the cooking pot.

3. To give the stock more flavor, add more mushroom water. Add the remaining ingredients, excluding the greens, and simmer for an additional 15 minutes, or until the squash is tender.

4. Include the chopped greens and allow them to wilt before serving. Serve with Tabasco sauce if you like it spicy.

Nutritional Info: Calories: 1191 Fat: 56g Carbs: 158g Protein: 19g

Peppery Soup with Tomato

Preparation Time: 2 minutes
Cooking time: 35 minutes
Servings: 2
Ingredients:

- 2 red bell peppers
- 4 beef tomatoes
- 1 sweet onion, chopped
- 1 garlic clove, chopped
- 3 cups homemade chicken broth
- 2 habanero chilis, stems removed and chopped
- 2 tablespoon extra-virgin olive oil

Directions:

1. Set the broiler to medium-high heat and cook the bell peppers for 10 minutes, flipping them halfway through.
2. Use a sharp knife to make a tiny x in the bottom of each tomato and boil water in a skillet over medium-high heat.
3. After cooking, transfer the pepper to a different dish and cover it. The tomatoes should be blanched in boiling water for 20 seconds.
4. Take off and submerge yourself in icy water. With the fluids saved, peel and cut the tomatoes.

5. In a skillet over medium-high heat, cook the onion, garlic, chili, and 2 tablespoons of oil while stirring for 8 to 10 minutes, or until golden.

6. Combine the broth, peppers, and tomatoes with their juices; add to the onions; cover; and simmer for 10 to 15 minutes, or until the chicken is cooked through. Blend until smooth, then serve.

Nutritional Info: Calories: 741 Fat: 32g Carbs: 30g Protein: 82g

Moroccan Inspired Lentil Soup

Preparation Time: 5 minutes
Cooking time: 40 minutes
Servings: 2
Ingredients:

- 2 tablespoon extra-virgin olive oil
- 1 yellow onion, diced
- 1 carrot, diced
- 1 clove of minced garlic, diced
- 1 teaspoon cumin, ground
- ½ teaspoon ginger, ground
- 2 tablespoon low-fat Greek yogurt
- ½ teaspoon turmeric, ground
- ½ teaspoon red chili flakes
- 1 can tomatoes, chopped
- 1 cup dried yellow lentils, soaked
- 5 cups of low salt vegetable stock or homemade chicken stock
- 1 lemon

Directions:

1. In a large pan over medium-high heat, heat the oil. The onion and carrot should be sautéed for 5 to 6 minutes, or until tender and beginning to brown.
2. Include the turmeric, cumin, chili flakes, garlic, and ginger, and simmer for 2 minutes.
3. Add the tomatoes and simmer for 15 to 20 minutes, scraping up any browned pieces from the pan's bottom as you go.
4. Add the lentils and stock, increase the heat, and bring to a boil. Then, reduce the heat, cover the pan, and simmer for 10 minutes.
5. Serve Greek yogurt with a lemon slice on the side.

Nutritional Info: Calories: 1048 Fat: 53g Carbs: 128g Protein: 19g

Classic Vegetarian Tagine

Preparation Time: 10 minutes
Cooking time: 45 minutes
Servings: 2
Ingredients:

- 2 tablespoon coconut oil
- 1 onion, diced
- 1 parsnip, peeled and diced
- 2 cloves of garlic
- 1 teaspoon cumin, ground
- ½ teaspoon ginger, ground
- ½ teaspoon cinnamon, ground
- ¼ teaspoon cayenne pepper
- 3 tablespoon tomato paste
- 1 sweet potato, peeled & diced
- 1 purple potato, peeled & diced
- 4 baby carrots, peeled & diced

- 4 cups low-salt vegetable stock
- 2 cups kale leaves
- 2 tablespoons lemon juice
- ¼ cup cilantro, roughly chopped
- handful of almonds, toasted

Directions:

1. In a large pot, heat the oil over medium-high heat while softening the onion. For 10 minutes, or until golden brown, add the parsnip.
2. Include the cayenne, tomato paste, ginger, cinnamon, cumin, and coriander. Cook for 2 minutes, or until a lovely aroma appears.
3. Stir in the stock, purple potatoes, carrots, and sweet potatoes before bringing to a boil. Reduce the heat, then simmer for 20 minutes.
4. Add the kale and lemon juice, and simmer for an additional 2 minutes, or until the leaves are just beginning to wilt. To serve, garnish with the cilantro and nuts.

Nutritional Info: Calories: 1115 Fat: 51g Carbs: 150g Protein: 19g

Homemade Warm and Chunky Chicken Soup

Preparation Time: 7 minutes
Cooking time: 40 minutes
Servings: 4
Ingredients:

- 1 whole free-range chicken, cooked and no giblets
- 1 bay leaf
- 5 cups of homemade chicken broth/water
- 1 onion, chopped
- 2 stalks of celery, sliced
- 3 carrots, chopped and peeled

- 2 parsnips, chopped and peeled
- sprinkle of pepper

Directions:

1. Place all the ingredients, excluding the pepper, in a large saucepan and bring to a boil over high heat. Once it begins to boil, reduce the heat and let the chicken simmer for 30 minutes, or until it is scalding hot.
2. Take the chicken out of the pan and set it on a cutting board. Remove the skin and bones from the bird and slice as much flesh as you can.
3. Return it to the stove and either serve it immediately as a chunky soup or let it cool and then puree it before serving.
4. Season with black pepper and serve alone or with your preferred whole-grain bread. To savor the flavors of the soup, add the bread to the pot 20 minutes before it's finished cooking.

Nutritional Info: Calories: 101 Fat: 1g Carbs: 22g Protein: 7g

Indian Curried Stew with Lentil and Spinach

Preparation Time: 5 minutes
Cooking time: 30 minutes
Servings: 2
Ingredients:

- 1 tablespoon extra-virgin olive oil
- 1 tablespoon curry powder
- 1 cup homemade chicken or vegetable stock
- 1 cup red lentils, soaked
- 1 onion, chopped
- 2 cups butternut squash, cooked peeled, and chopped

- 1 cup spinach
- 2 garlic cloves, minced
- 1 tablespoon cilantro, finely chopped

Directions:

1. In a large saucepan, add the oil, minced garlic, and onion, and sauté for 5 minutes over low heat. Cook the onions for 5 minutes after adding the curry powder and ginger.
2. Add the broth and cook over high heat until it begins to boil. Add the spinach, lentils, and squash, turn down the heat, and simmer for an additional 20 minutes.
3. Add fresh cilantro to the dish and add pepper to taste.

Nutritional Info: Calories: 1022 Fat: 19g Carbs: 91g Protein: 123g

Soulful Roasted Vegetable Soup

Preparation Time: 10 minutes
Cooking time: 30 minutes
Servings: 2
Ingredients:

- 2 medium carrots, peeled
- 1 cup baby Brussels sprouts
- 1 rib celery
- ¼ medium head cabbage
- 2 teaspoons fine Himalayan salt, divided
- 2 tablespoons coconut oil
- 2 cups bone broth
- ½ medium Hass avocado, peeled, pitted, and sliced
- 1 green onion, minced
- 4 sprigs fresh cilantro, minced

Directions:
1. Turn on the oven to 400°F.
2. Separate out all of the vegetables on a sheet pan and chop them all into little pieces. Add 1 teaspoon of salt, then combine with coconut oil. Roast for 30 minutes.
3. While the vegetables are roasting, warm the broth in a pot over medium heat.
4. When the veggies are prepared, divide them into two serving dishes. Add the remaining teaspoon of salt, along with the avocado, green onion, and cilantro. Allocate the soup among the bowls.
5. Serve right away. For up to 4 days, keep leftovers in the refrigerator in an airtight container.

Nutritional Info: Calories: 276 Fat: 23g Carbs: 19gProtein: 6g

Corn Chowder

Preparation Time: 20 minutes
Cooking time: 50 minutes
Servings: 4
Ingredients:

- 3 tablespoons avocado oil
- 2 cups onions, diced
- 3 cups bone broth
- 2 cups cauliflower pearls
- ¾ cup coconut cream
- 2 teaspoons black pepper, ground
- 1 teaspoon fine Himalayan salt
- ½ teaspoon cumin, ground
- ½ teaspoon nutmeg, ground
- 2 tablespoons nutritional yeast

- Leaves from fresh thyme sprig
- 2 tablespoons Garlic Confit

Directions:

1. Heat a medium-sized saucepan on the stovetop. When the avocado oil is heated, pour it in and then add the chopped onion. Cover the pan and reduce the heat to medium-low.
2. Cook for 20 minutes, stirring halfway through. The onions must be tender and sweet; therefore, they should be lightly fried but not crunchy.
3. Include the spices, coconut cream, cauliflower, and broth. Stir well before simmering. Simmer for 20 to 30 minutes, stirring once and again.
4. When the soup has been reduced by a third and the onion and cauliflower bits are poking through the liquid, it is time to add cream.
5. Pour half of the soup into a blender. Don't only pour broth into the blender; be sure to include lots of cauliflower and onions as well.
6. After puréeing everything until it is silky smooth, return it to the stove and whisk everything together to make a creamy soup that is flecked with soft cauliflower pearls and fragrant onions.
7. Before serving, garnish with the thyme and garlic confit. For up to 5 days in the refrigerator or 30 days in the freezer, place leftovers in an airtight container. Reheat on the stovetop by bringing it to a simmer.

Nutritional Info: Calories: 202 Fat: 13g Carbs: 14g Protein: 12g

Egg Drop Soup

Preparation Time: 5 minutes
Cooking time: 25 minutes
Servings: 4

Ingredients:

- 2 tablespoons sesame oil, toasted
- 2-inch piece fresh ginger, peeled
- 4 cloves garlic, peeled
- 4 cups bone broth
- 1 tablespoon coconut aminos
- 1 tablespoon fish sauce
- Pinch of fine Himalayan salt
- 4 large eggs, whisked
- 2 green onions, sliced,
- 4 sprigs fresh cilantro, minced,

Directions:

1. In a 6- or 8-quart saucepan, heat the sesame oil over medium heat. Stir in the ginger and garlic until they start to lighten in color.
2. Include the salt, fish sauce, coconut aminos, and broth. Cook for 20 minutes with the lid on after bringing it to a gentle simmer.
3. Slowly drizzle the eggs into the soup while stirring it so that they cook quickly in ribbons as soon as they contact the broth.
4. Top with cilantro and green onions for garnish, then serve hot. For up to five days, keep leftovers in the refrigerator in an airtight container.

Nutritional Info: Calories: 185 Fat: 12g Carbs: 4g Protein: 16g

SNACK RECIPES

Okra Fries

Preparation time: 15 minutes
Cooking time: 35 minutes
Servings: 4

Ingredients:

- 2 tablespoons olive oil, divided
- 3 tablespoons creole seasoning
- ½ teaspoon ground turmeric
- 1 teaspoon water
- 1-pound okra, trimmed and slit in the middle

Directions:

1. Set the oven to 450 degrees Fahrenheit. A foil-lined baking sheet should be greased with 1 tablespoon of oil.
2. Combine water, turmeric, and creole seasoning in a bowl. Okra slits should be filled with the turmeric mixture.
3. Arrange the okra in a single layer on the prepared baking sheet. 30 to 35 minutes of baking time, flipping once during the middle.

Nutritional Info: Calories: 119 Fat: 6.98g Carbohydrates: 12.43g Protein: 2.51g

Potato Sticks

Preparation time: 15 minutes
Cooking time: 10 minutes
Servings: 2
Ingredients:

- 1 large russet potato, peeled and cut into 1/8-inch thick sticks lengthwise
- 10 curry leaves
- ¼ teaspoon ground turmeric
- ¼ teaspoon red chili powder
- Salt, to taste
- 1 tbsp essential olive oil

Directions:

1. Set the oven to 400 degrees Fahrenheit. Use parchment paper to line two baking sheets.
2. Combine all the ingredients in a large dish and stir to evenly coat. Place the amalgamation in a single layer on the prepared baking sheets.
3. Cook for about 10 minutes. Serve right away.

Nutritional Info: Calories: 175 Fat: 3.21g Carbohydrates: 33.78g Protein: 4.06g

Zucchini Chips

Preparation time: 15 minutes
Cooking time: 15 minutes
Servings: 2
Ingredients:

- 1 medium zucchini, cut into thin slices
- 1/8 teaspoon ground turmeric
- 1/8 teaspoon ground cumin
- Salt, to taste
- 2 teaspoons essential olive oil

Directions:

1. Set the oven to 400 degrees Fahrenheit. Use parchment paper to line two baking sheets.
2. Combine all the ingredients in a large bowl and toss to evenly coat. Place the mixture in a single layer onto the prepared baking sheets.
3. Bake for roughly 10 to 15 minutes. Serve right away.

Nutritional Info: Calories: 20 Fat: 2g Carbohydrates: 0.37g Protein: 0.21g

Beet Chips

Preparation time: 15 minutes
Cooking time: 20 minutes
Servings: 2

Ingredients:

- 1 beetroot, trimmed, peeled, and sliced thinly
- 1 teaspoon garlic, minced
- 1 tablespoon nutritional yeast
- ½ teaspoon red chili powder
- 2 teaspoons coconut oil, melted

Directions:

1. Set the oven to 375 degrees Fahrenheit. Use parchment paper to cover a baking sheet.
2. Combine all the ingredients in a large bowl and stir to evenly coat.
3. Spoon the mixture, in a single layer, onto the prepared baking sheet.
4. Bake for about twenty minutes, turning the dish once in the middle. Serve right away.

Nutritional Info: Calories: 80 Fat: 4.5g Carbohydrates: 6g Protein: 3g

Spinach Chips

Preparation time: 10 minutes
Cooking time: 8 minutes
Servings: 1
Ingredients:

- 2 cups fresh spinach leaves
- Few drops of extra-virgin olive oil
- Salt, to taste
- Italian seasoning, to taste

Directions:
1. Set the oven's temperature to 325 F. Use parchment paper to cover a baking sheet.
2. Place spinach leaves in a large bowl and top with oil. Rub the spinach leaves in your hands until they are completely covered in oil.
3. Place the leaves in a single layer on the prepared baking sheet. For about 8 minutes, bake. Serve right away.

Nutritional Info: Calories: 14 Fat: 4.5g Carbohydrates: 2.18g Protein: 1.72g

Sweet & Tangy Seeds Crackers

Preparation time: 15 minutes
Cooking time: 12 hours

Servings: 10
Ingredients:

- 2 cups water
- 1 cup sunflower seeds
- 1 cup flaxseeds
- 1 tablespoon fresh ginger, chopped
- 1 teaspoon raw honey
- ¼ cup freshly squeezed lemon juice
- 1 teaspoon ground turmeric
- Salt, to taste

Directions:

1. Soak sunflower seeds and flaxseeds in water in a bowl for about an overnight period. Take out the seeds.
2. Pulse the remaining ingredients, along with the soaked seeds, in a food processor until thoroughly combined. The dehydrator should be set to 115 degrees F. Put parchment paper that hasn't been bleached on a dehydrator tray.
3. Evenly distribute the mix over the dehydrator tray that has been prepared. How many crackers should you score with a knife? For about 12 hours, dehydrate.

Nutritional Info: Calories: 176 Fat: 14.32g Carbohydrates: 8.97g Protein: 6.05g

Plantain Chips

Preparation time: quarter-hour
Cooking time: 10 min
Servings: 1
Ingredients:

- 1 plantain, peeled and sliced
- ½ teaspoon ground turmeric
- Salt, to taste
- 1 teaspoon coconut oil, melted

Directions:

1. Combine all the ingredients in a large bowl and toss to combine. Place half of the mixture in an enormous oiled basin. 3 minutes on high in the microwave
2. Next, reduce the container's volume to 50% and microwave for 2 minutes. Apply the remaining plantain mixture in the same manner.

Nutritional Info: Calories: 222 Fat: 4.83g Carbohydrates: 48.98g Protein: 1.36g

Quinoa & Seeds Crackers

Preparation time: 15 minutes
Cooking time: 20 or so minutes
Servings: 6
Ingredients:

- 3 tablespoons water
- 1 tablespoon chia seeds
- 3 tablespoons sunflower seeds
- 1 tablespoon quinoa flour
- 1 teaspoon ground turmeric
- Pinch of ground cinnamon
- Salt, to taste

Directions:

1. Set the oven to 345 degrees Fahrenheit. Use parchment paper to cover a baking sheet.
2. Place the chia seeds in a basin with water and let them soak for about 30 minutes.
3. Add the other ingredients and thoroughly combine them after fifteen minutes.
4. Disperse the mixture on a baking sheet that has been prepared. Bake for about 20 minutes.

Nutritional Info: Calories: 34 Fat: 2.38g Carbohydrates: 2.35g Protein: 1.21g

Apple Leather

Preparation time: 15 minutes
Cooking time: 12 hours, 25 minutes
Servings: 4
Ingredients:

- 1 cup water
- 8 cups apples, peeled, cored, and chopped
- 1 tablespoon ground cinnamon
- 2 tablespoons freshly squeezed lemon juice

Directions:

1. Heat water and apples in a large pan over low heat. Stirring periodically, simmer for 10 minutes. Take the pan off the heat and let it sit aside to cool somewhat.
2. Add the apple mixture to a blender and process until smooth. Return the mixture to the pan and lower the heat to low.
3. Add fresh lemon juice and cinnamon; simmer for about 10 minutes. The easiest way to smooth the mixture before transferring it to dehydrator trays is with the back of a spoon.

4. Adjust the dehydrator to 135 degrees Fahrenheit. Dehydrate for ten to twelve hours. Cut the apple leather into rectangles of the same size. Making fruit rolls now requires rolling each rectangle.

Nutritional Info: Calories: 120 Fat: 0.41g Carbohydrates: 32.2g Protein: 0.67g

Roasted Cashews

Preparation time: 5 minutes
Cooking time: 20 or so minutes
Servings: 16
Ingredients:

- 2 cups cashews
- 2 teaspoons raw honey
- 1½ teaspoons smoked paprika
- ½ teaspoon chili flakes
- Salt, to taste
- 1 tablespoon freshly squeezed lemon juice
- 1 teaspoon organic olive oil

Directions:

1. Set the oven to 350 degrees Fahrenheit. Using parchment paper, line a baking pan. Add all the ingredients to a bowl and combine well by tossing.
2. Spread the cashew mixture in a single layer in a baking dish. Roast for about 20 minutes, turning once in the middle.
3. Take the dish out of the oven and set it aside to cool before serving. These roasted cashews can be stored in an airtight container.

Nutritional Info: Calories: 200 Fat: 17.13g Carbohydrates: 10.65g Protein: 3.93g

Roasted Pumpkin Seeds

Preparation time: 10 minutes
Cooking time: 20 minutes
Servings: 4
Ingredients:

- 1 cup pumpkin seeds, washed and dried
- 2 teaspoons garam masala
- 1/3 teaspoon red chili powder
- ¼ teaspoon ground turmeric
- Salt, to taste
- 3 tablespoons coconut oil, melted
- ½ tablespoon fresh lemon juice

Directions:

1. Set the oven to 350 degrees Fahrenheit. Add all the ingredients to a bowl, excluding the lemon juice, and toss to combine.
2. Immediately place the almond mixture on a baking sheet. Roast for about twenty minutes, occasionally flipping.
3. Take the dish out of the oven and set it aside to cool before serving. Serve after drizzling with freshly squeezed lemon juice.

Nutritional Info: Calories: 259 Fat: 24.71g Carbohydrates: 4.72g Protein: 8.86g

Spiced Popcorn

Preparation time: 5 minutes

Cooking time: 2 minutes
Servings: 2-3
Ingredients:

- 3 tablespoons coconut oil
- ½ cup popping corn
- 1 tbsp olive oil
- 1 teaspoon ground turmeric
- ¼ teaspoon garlic
- Salt, to taste

Directions:

1. Melt coconut oil in a pan over medium-high heat. Cover the pan tightly after adding the popped corn.
2. Cook, occasionally shaking the pan, for about 1-2 minutes, or until corn kernels start to pop.
3. Remove from the heat and place immediately in a sizable heatproof bowl. Mix well after adding spices and essential olive oil.

Nutritional Info: Calories: 261 Fat: 19.45g Carbohydrates: 21.29g Protein: 2.3g

DESSERT RECIPES

Café-Style Fudge

Preparation Time: 10 minutes + chilling time
Cooking time: 0 minutes
Servings: 6
Ingredients:

- 1 tablespoon instant coffee granules
- 4 tablespoons confectioners' Swerve
- 4 tablespoons cocoa powder
- 1 stick butter
- 1/2 teaspoon vanilla extract

Directions:

1. Use a low speed to combine the butter and swerve. Continue blending after adding the vanilla, cocoa powder, and instant coffee granules.
2. Pour the batter onto a baking sheet lined with foil. For two to three hours, refrigerate. Enjoy!

Nutritional Info: Calories 144 Fat 15.5g Carbs 2.1g Protein 0.8g

Coconut and Seed Porridge

Preparation Time: 15 minutes
Cooking time: 0 minutes
Servings: 2
Ingredients:

- 6 tablespoons coconut flour
- 1/2 cup canned coconut milk
- 4 tablespoons double cream
- 2 tablespoons flaxseed meal
- 1 tablespoon pumpkin seeds, ground

Directions:

1. Simmer all of the ingredients listed above in a saucepan over medium heat. Add your preferred keto sweetener.
2. Distribute the porridge among bowls and savor!

Nutritional Info: Calories 300 Fat 25.1g Carbs 8g Protein 4.9g

Pecan and Lime Cheesecake

Preparation Time: 30 minutes + chilling time
Cooking time: 0 minutes
Servings: 10
Ingredients:

- 1 cup coconut flakes
- 20 ounces mascarpone cheese, room temperature
- 1 ½ cups pecan meal
- 1/2 cup xylitol
- 3 tablespoons key lime juice

Directions:

1. In a mixing bowl, combine the pecan meal, 1/4 cup of xylitol, and coconut flakes. Line a springform pan with parchment paper and press the crust into it. For 30 minutes, freeze.
2. Use an electric mixer to combine 1/4 cup of xylitol with the mascarpone cheese. The key is that lime juice should be beaten in,

and vanilla extract is optional.

3. Place the prepared crust on top of the filling. In your refrigerator, let it cool for about three hours. Good appetite!

Nutritional Info: Calories 296 Fat 20g Carbs 6g Protein 21g

Rum Butter Cookies

Preparation Time: 10 minutes + chilling time
Cooking time: 0 minutes
Servings: 12

Ingredients:

- 1/2 cup coconut butter
- 1 teaspoon rum extract
- 4 cups almond meal
- 1 stick butter
- 1/2 cup confectioners' Swerve

Directions:

1. Melt the butter and coconut butter. Add the Swerve and rum extract and stir. The almond meal should then be added and combined.

2. After rolling, put the balls on a cookie sheet lined with parchment paper. Place it there until you're ready to serve, then refrigerate.

Nutritional Info: Calories 400 Fat 40g Carbs 4.9g Protein 5.4g

Fluffy Chocolate Chip Cookies

Preparation Time: 10 minutes + chilling time
Cooking time: 0 minutes
Servings: 10

Ingredients:

- 1/2 cup almond meal
- 4 tablespoons double cream
- 1/2 cup sugar-free chocolate chips
- 2 cups coconut, unsweetened and shredded
- 1/2 cup monk fruit syrup

Directions:

1. In a mixing bowl, stir together all of the ingredients listed above. Make bite-sized balls of the batter.
2. With the aid of a fork or your hand, flatten the balls. Place it there until you're ready to serve, then refrigerate.

Nutritional Info: Calories 104 Fat 9.5g Carbs 4.1g Protein 2.1g

Chewy Almond Blondies

Preparation Time: 55 minutes
Cooking time: 0 minutes
Servings: 10

Ingredients:

- 1/2 cup sugar-free bakers' chocolate, chopped into small chunks
- 1/4 cup erythritol
- 2 tablespoons coconut oil
- 1 cup almond meal
- 1 cup almond butter

Directions:

1. Cream together almond butter, almond meal, and erythritol in a mixing bowl.
2. Evenly press the mixture onto a baking sheet lined with foil. For

30 to 35 minutes, freeze.
3. To make the glaze, melt the baker's chocolate and coconut oil. Spread the glaze over your cake and place it in the freezer to set the chocolate. Cut into bars, then eat!

Nutritional Info: Calories 234 Fat 25.1g Carbs 3.6g Protein 1.7g

Light Greek Cheesecake

Preparation Time: 15 minutes
Cooking time: 35 minutes
Servings: 6
Ingredients:

- 10 ounces whipped Greek yogurt cream cheese
- 6 tablespoons butter, melted
- 2 cups confectioner's Swerve
- 2 eggs
- 2 cups almond meal

Directions:

1. Set your oven's temperature to 325 degrees Fahrenheit. Press the crust mixture into a lightly buttered springform pan by combining the butter and almond meal.
2. Combine all ingredients by thoroughly blending the Greek-style yogurt with confectioners' Swerve. One at a time, fold in the eggs and thoroughly combine everything before adding the next.
3. Smother the crust with the contents. Bake for approximately 35 minutes in a preheated oven, or until the center is still jiggly. As it cools, your cheesecake will continue to solidify. Good appetite!

Nutritional Info: Calories 471 Fat 45g Carbs 6.9g Protein 11.5g

Fluffy Chocolate Crepes

Preparation Time: 20 minutes
Cooking time: 8 minutes
Servings: 2
Ingredients:

- 1/4 cup coconut milk, unsweetened
- 2 eggs, beaten
- 1/2 cup coconut flour
- 1 tablespoon unsweetened cocoa powder
- 2 tablespoons coconut oil, melted

Directions:

1. Combine the coconut flour, cocoa powder, and 1/2 teaspoon baking soda well in a mixing bowl.
2. Combine the eggs, coconut milk, and other ingredients in another bowl. Add the flour mixture and well blend it with the egg mixture.
3. Heat 1 tablespoon of the coconut oil in a frying pan until it is sizzling. Pour in half of the batter and cook for 2 to 3 minutes on each side in the frying pan.
4. Fry another crepe for around five minutes, using the last tablespoon of coconut oil that has melted. Serve with the keto filling of your choice. Good appetite!

Nutritional Info: Calories 330 Fat 31.9g Carbs 7.1g Protein 7.3g

Crispy Peanut Fudge Squares

Preparation Time: 1 hour
Cooking time: 0 minutes
Servings: 10

Ingredients:

- 1/2 cup peanuts, toasted and coarsely chopped
- 1 vanilla paste
- 2 tablespoons Monk fruit powder
- 1 stick butter
- 1/3 cup coconut oil

Directions:

1. Melt the coconut oil, butter, and vanilla. Monk fruit powder should be added and thoroughly mixed in.
2. Fill the ice cube trays with the chopped peanuts. Over the peanuts, pour the batter. Place it there for approximately an hour in the freezer. Good appetite!

Nutritional Info: Calories 218 Fat 21.2g Carbs 5.1g Protein 3.8g

Almond Butter Cookies

Preparation Time: 15 minutes + chilling time
Cooking time: 5 minutes
Servings: 8

Ingredients:

- 1 ½ cups almond butter
- 1/2 cup sugar-free chocolate, cut into chunks
- 1/2 cup double cream
- 1/2 cup Monk fruit powder
- 3 cups pork rinds, crushed

Directions:

1. Melt the almond butter and monk fruit powder; if desired, add the crushed pork rinds and vanilla.

2. Disperse the mixture onto a cookie sheet, then put it in the fridge.

3. Spread the chocolate layer over the first layer after heating the chocolate and double cream in the microwave. Place it there until you're ready to serve, then refrigerate. Enjoy!

Nutritional Info: Calories 322 Fat 28.9g Carbs 3.4g Protein 13.9g

Basic Almond Cupcakes

Preparation Time: 15 minutes
Cooking time: 18-20 minutes
Servings: 9

Ingredients:

- 1 cup almond milk, unsweetened
- 2 tablespoons coconut oil
- 1/2 cup almond meal
- 1/4 cup Swerve
- 3 eggs

Directions:

1. Combine all of the ingredients listed above well. Cupcake liners should be used to line a muffin pan.

Put the batter in the muffin tin by spooning.

3. Bake in the 350°F preheated oven for 18 to 20 minutes, or until a toothpick inserted into the center of the cake comes out dry and clean. Enjoy!

Nutritional Info: Calories 134 Fat 11.6g Carbs 2.9g Protein 5.4g

Blueberry Cheesecake Bowl

Preparation Time: 10 minutes + chilling time
Cooking time: 0 minutes
Servings: 8

Ingredients:

- 2 cups cream cheese
- 1/2 cup blueberries
- 1/2 teaspoon coconut extract
- 6 tablespoons pecans, chopped
- 1/4 cup coconut cream

Directions:

1. Cream cheese and coconut cream should be thoroughly combined in Step 1.
2. Continue mixing after adding the pecans, 1/4 cup of blueberries, and coconut extract. For two to three hours, refrigerate. Serve with the remaining 1/4 cup of blueberries as a garnish. Enjoy!

Nutritional Info: Calories 244 Fat 24.2g Carbs 4.7g Protein 3.7g

SMOOTHIES RECIPES

Cacao Berry Smoothie

Preparation Time: 5 minutes
Cooking time: 0 minutes
Servings: 1
Ingredients:

- 1 cup almond milk
- 1 banana
- 1 cup fresh baby spinach
- ½ cup filtered water
- 1 cup raspberries
- 1 tbsp. honey
- 3 tbsp. cacao powder
- ice
- cacao nibs

Directions:

1. Place all ingredients in a blender and process until smooth. Add cocoa nibs as a garnish if you'd like. Sip some alcohol and unwind.

Nutritional Info: Calories: 170 Carbs: 27g Fat: 3g Protein: 5g

Greek Yogurt Smoothie

Preparation Time: 5 minutes
Cooking time: 0 minutes
Servings: 1
Ingredients:

- 1 cup almond milk
- ¼ cup baby spinach
- ½ cup plain Greek yogurt
- ¼ cup blueberries
- pinch of ground cinnamon
- 1 tbsp. almond butter
- cardamom
- pistachios
- 3-4 ice cubes

Directions:

1. Place all ingredients in a blender, and pulse until combined and smooth.

Nutritional Info: Calories: 392 Carbs: 57g Fat: 10g Protein: 25g

Pineapple Smoothie

Preparation Time: 5 minutes
Cooking time: 0 minutes
Servings: 1
Ingredients:

- 1 cup brewed green tea
- 1 cup frozen pineapple chunks
- 2 cups spinach
- ½ cup frozen mango chunks
- 2/3 cup cucumber
- ½ of a medium banana
- ¼ tsp. ground turmeric

- 1/2" fresh ginger
- 3 mint leaves
- 1 tbsp. chia seeds
- 1 scoop protein powder
- 4–5 ice cubes

Directions:

1. Except for the chia seeds, combine all the ingredients in a powerful blender.
2. To prevent the chia seeds from sticking to the blender container, add them toward the end of the blending process.
3. Add ice cubes and blend the smoothie until the desired consistency is reached if you prefer a thicker smoothie.

Nutritional Info: Calories: 331 Carbs: 77g Fat: 4g Protein: 0g

Blueberry Banana Smoothie

Preparation Time: 5 minutes
Cooking time: 0 minutes
Servings: 2

Ingredients:

- 2 cups frozen banana chunks
- 1 tsp. almond butter
- 1 cup frozen blueberries
- 1 tsp. ground flax seed
- 1¼ cups almond milk

Directions:

1. Using a powerful blender, puree frozen blueberries, frozen bananas, ground flaxseed, almond butter, and almond milk until

smooth.
2. Transfer the smoothie to glasses, then serve immediately.
Nutritional Info: Calories: 175 Carbs: 40g Fat: 6g Protein: 4g

Blueberry Pie Smoothie

Preparation Time: 5 minutes
Cooking time: 0 minutes
Servings: 3
Ingredients:

- 1 cup plain Greek yogurt
- 1 cup frozen banana chunks
- ¾ tsp. lemon zest
- ½ cup rolled oats
- 3 cups frozen blueberries
- 1½ cups almond milk
- 1/8 cup pure maple syrup
- ½ tsp. cinnamon

Directions:
1 .In a powerful blender, combine all the ingredients and pulse until smooth
Nutrition: Calories: 400 Carbs: 36g Fat: 12g Protein: 28g

Strawberry Banana Smoothie

Preparation Time: 5 minutes
Cooking time: 0 minutes
Servings: 3

Ingredients:

- 4 cups frozen strawberries
- 1 cup milk of choice
- 1 cup frozen banana chunks

Directions:
1. Add milk to the blender on your powerful machine.
2. Sprinkle frozen bananas and strawberries on top of the milk.
3. Blend at high speed until the mixture is flawless.

Nutritional Info: Calories: 120 Carbs: 29g Fat: 0g Protein: 1g

Mango Pineapple Smoothie

Preparation Time: 5 minutes
Cooking time: 0 minutes
Servings: 1
Ingredients:

- ½ cup frozen mango chunks
- ¾ cup almond milk
- 1 clementine, peeled
- 1 tsp. ground flax seed
- ½ cup frozen pineapple chunks
- ½ cup frozen banana chunks

Directions:
1. In a powerful blender, combine all the ingredients and blend until completely smooth.
2. Serve immediately.

Nutritional Info: Calories: 245 Carbs: 44g Fat: 2g Protein: 6g

Avocado Smoothie

Preparation Time: 5 minutes
Cooking time: 0 minutes
Servings: 1
Ingredients:

- 1 avocado
- 1 cup frozen pineapple
- 2 tsp. honey
- 1/3 cup vanilla Greek yogurt
- ½ cup almond milk
- 1 - 2 cups of ice

Directions:
1. Place all ingredients—except the ice—in a powerful blender and whirl until smooth.
2. Add the ice and blend until the desired consistency is achieved. Enjoy.

Nutritional Info: Calories: 71 Carbs: 3g Fat: 6g Protein: 1g

Strawberry Smoothie

Preparation Time: 5 minutes
Cooking time: 0 minutes
Servings: 3
Ingredients:

- 2 lbs. fresh strawberries
- ¼ cup milk
- 1 cup plain Greek yogurt

- 1/3 cup rolled oats
- 1/3 cup frozen pineapple
- 2 - 3 cups ice

Directions:
1. Place all of the ingredients in a blender and blend until well-combined.
2. Adjust the amount of ice to get the desired consistency.

Nutritional Info: Calories: 375 Carbs: 84g Fat: 2g Protein: 1g

Beet Smoothie

Preparation Time: 5 minutes
Cooking time: 0 minutes
Servings: 1
Ingredients:

- 1 small beet
- 1 ½ cups frozen mixed berries
- 1 apple
- ¼ cup plain Greek yogurt
- 2/3 cup almond milk
- 1 tsp. honey

Directions:
1. Place all of the ingredients in a blender and blend until well-combined.
2. Adjust the amount of ice to get the desired consistency.

Nutritional Info: Calories: 205 Carbs: 0g Fat: 2g Protein: 4g

Turmeric Smoothie

Preparation Time: 5 minutes
Cooking time: 0 minutes
Servings: 1
Ingredients:

- 1 tsp. turmeric paste
- 1 cup frozen pineapple
- 1½ cups cold water
- 1 tsp. coconut oil
- 1 cup frozen mango
- 1 tsp. fresh ginger

Directions:
1. Place all of the ingredients in a blender and blend until well-combined.
2. Adjust the amount of ice to get the desired consistency.

Nutritional Info: Calories: 323 Carbs: 44g Fat: 18g Protein: 3g

Spinach Smoothie

Preparation Time: 5 minutes
Cooking time: 0 minutes
Servings: 2
Ingredients:

- 2 cups fresh spinach
- 1 large orange
- 1 cup almond milk

- 1 large banana
- 2 tbsp. ground flaxseed meal
- ice

Directions:
1. Place all of the ingredients in a blender and blend until well-combined.
2. Adjust the amount of ice to get the desired consistency.

Nutritional Info: Calories: 316 Carbs: 52g Fat: 6g Protein: 21g

Mint Chocolate Chip Smoothie

Preparation Time: 5 minutes
Cooking time: 0 minutes
Servings: 2
Ingredients:

- 2 medium frozen bananas
- ¼ cup fresh mint leaves
- 1 cup almond milk
- ¼ cup chocolate chips

Directions:

1. Place all of the ingredients in a blender and blend until well-combined.

Nutritional Info: Calories: 140 Carbs: 42g Fat: 22g Protein: 17g

Chocolate Protein Smoothie

Preparation Time: 5 minutes
Cooking time: 0 minutes
Servings: 1
Ingredients:

- 1 ½ cups frozen strawberries
- 3 tbsp. fruit sweetener
- 1½ cups almond milk
- 3 tbsp. raw cacao powder
- 2 scoops unflavored protein

Directions:

1. Place all of the ingredients in a blender and blend until well-combined.

Nutritional Info: Calories: 210 Carbs: 19g Fat: 5g Protein: 24g

Peach Kiwi Green Smoothie

Preparation Time: 5 minutes
Cooking time: 0 minutes
Servings: 1
Ingredients:

- ¼ cup coconut milk
- 1 handful spinach leaves
- 1 kiwi, peeled
- 1 large, ripe banana
- 10 slices frozen peaches

Directions:

1. Banana, peach slices, coconut milk, kiwi, and spinach leaves should all be thoroughly blended in step 1.

2. To achieve the ideal consistency, if it's too thick, thin it out with a little almond milk.

Nutritional Info: Calories: 48 Carbs: 12g Fat: 0g Protein: 0g

STAPLES, SAUCES AND DRESSINGS

Savory Herbed Quinoa

Preparation Time: 10 minutes
Cooking time: 20 minutes
Servings: 3 ½ cups
Ingredients:

- 1 cup quinoa, rinsed
- 2 cups vegetable broth
- 1½ tablespoons olive oil
- Juice of ½ lemon
- ½ teaspoon salt
- ½ teaspoon freshly ground black pepper
- ½ cup chopped fresh parsley
- ½ cup chopped fresh basil
- 2 scallions, chopped

Directions:

1. Put the quinoa and broth in a pan and heat them up until they boil. In order for the liquid to be absorbed and the quinoa to appear fluffy, lower the heat to medium-low, cover the pan, and simmer it for 15 to 20 minutes.
2. Turn off the heat and let the food sit, covered, for an additional 10 minutes. Add the olive oil, lemon juice, salt, pepper, parsley, basil, and scallions to the cooked quinoa in a big bowl. To incorporate, stir.

Nutritional Info: Calories: 175 Fat: 6g Protein: 5g Carbs: 25g

Honey-Lime Vinaigrette with Fresh Herbs

Preparation Time: 10 minutes
Cooking time: 0 minutes
Servings: 1 cup
Ingredients:

- Juice of 4 limes
- 3 tablespoons honey
- 2 tablespoons apple cider vinegar
- 2 tablespoons Dijon mustard
- 2 garlic cloves, minced
- 3 scallions, finely chopped
- ½ cup roughly chopped fresh cilantro

Directions:
1. Combine the lime juice, honey, vinegar, mustard, and garlic in a medium bowl. Stir in the cilantro and scallions after adding them.

Nutritional Info: Calories: 82 Fat: 1g Protein: 1g Carbs: 21g

Creamy Avocado Dressing

Preparation Time: 10 minutes
Cooking time: 0 minutes
Servings: 1 cup
Ingredients:

- 1 avocado, halved and pitted
- 1 tablespoon olive oil
- 2 teaspoons apple cider vinegar
- 1 garlic clove, peeled but whole

- Juice of 1 lemon
- ½ teaspoon onion powder
- 1 teaspoon maple syrup
- 1 teaspoon Dijon mustard
- ½ teaspoon salt
- ½ teaspoon freshly ground black pepper
- 10 tablespoons cold water

Directions:

1. Scoop the avocado into a blender or food processor. The mixture should be pulsed until it is smooth and creamy before adding the oil, vinegar, garlic, lemon juice, onion powder, maple syrup, mustard, salt, and pepper.
2. To make it thinner and more pourable, add as much water as necessary, 1 tablespoon at a time.

Nutritional Info: Calories: 105 Fat: 9g Protein: 1g Carbs: 7g

Avocado Crema

Preparation Time: 5 minutes
Cooking time: 0 minutes
Servings: 1 cup
Ingredients:

- 1 avocado, halved and pitted
- ¼ cup full-fat coconut milk
- Juice of 1 lime
- ¼ teaspoon salt
- ¼ cup fresh cilantro leaves

Directions:

1. Scoop the avocado into a blender or food processor. Pulse the mixture while adding the coconut milk, lime juice, salt, and cilantro to achieve a smooth, creamy, but still thick consistency.

Nutritional Info: Calories: 122 Fat: 11g Protein: 2g Carbs: 7g

Romesco

Preparation Time: 25 minutes
Cooking time: 45 minutes
Servings: 2 cups
Ingredients:

- 4 red bell peppers
- 5 tablespoons extra-virgin olive oil
- Kosher salt, to taste
- ¼ cup slivered almonds
- 2 garlic cloves, peeled and coarsely chopped
- 1 shallot, sliced
- ¼ teaspoon crushed red pepper
- 1 tablespoon sherry vinegar
- Freshly ground black pepper
- 2 tablespoons chopped mint
- ½ lemon

Directions:

1. Position a rack in the upper third of the oven and heat it to 400°F (205°C). Use parchment paper to cover a baking sheet. The bell peppers should be put in a medium bowl.
2. Drizzle the peppers with 1 tablespoon of the olive oil, add a big pinch of salt, and toss to evenly coat. Transfer the prepared baking sheet to the oven.

3. Roast the peppers for 15 minutes, then flip them over and roast them for a further 20 minutes, or until the peppers are tender and roasted and the skins are starting to peel away.

4. Place the peppers in a big bowl, wrap it up in plastic wrap, and set it aside for 10 minutes.

Remove the stems, skin, and seeds from the peppers after they are cool enough to handle. Roughly cut the flesh into strips, then set it aside.

6. Cook the almonds, stirring regularly, in a medium pan over medium heat for approximately 4 minutes, or until they start to appear and smell toasted. Put them on a platter to chill.

7. Add the garlic, shallot, and crushed red pepper to the same pan along with 2 tablespoons of the olive oil. Cook for approximately 2 minutes, stirring often, until the shallot softens and the garlic just starts to cook.

8. Insert the roasted peppers, shallot, and garlic into the food processor's bowl. Add the almonds after giving the processor a few pulses.

9. Add the remaining 2 tablespoons of olive oil, the sherry vinegar, 1/4 teaspoon salt, and a few grinds of pepper after pulsing a few more times and scraping the sides of the bowl as needed.

10. Continue processing until the romesco is consistently puréed but still has a little texture, much like a pesto sauce. Put it in a compact, airtight container.

11. Add the mint, a squeeze of lemon juice, and a few grinds of black pepper. If necessary, add more salt and pepper after tasting.

Nutritional Info: Calories: 210 Fat: 20g Protein: 2g Carbs: 6g

Creamy Turmeric Dressing

Preparation Time: 15 minutes
Cooking time: 0 minutes

Servings: 4-6
Ingredients:

- ¼ cup extra-virgin olive oil
- 2 tablespoons water
- 2 tablespoons freshly squeezed lemon juice
- 1½ tablespoons raw honey
- 1 tablespoon apple cider vinegar
- 1 teaspoon ground turmeric
- 1 teaspoon Dijon mustard
- ½ teaspoon ground ginger
- ¼ teaspoon sea salt
- Pinch freshly ground black pepper

Directions:

1. Mix the olive oil, water, lemon juice, honey, vinegar, mustard, ginger, salt, and pepper in a small bowl. To combine, whisk thoroughly.

Nutritional Info: Calories: 151 Fat: 14g Protein: 0g Carbs: 8g

Cherry-Peach Chutney with Mint

Preparation Time: 15 minutes
Cooking time: 0 minutes
Servings: 2 cups
Ingredients:

- 1 (10-ounce / 283-g) bag frozen no-added-sugar peach chunks, thawed, drained, coarsely chopped, juice reserved
- ½ medium red onion, diced

- ¼ cup dried cherries, coarsely chopped
- 2 tablespoons freshly squeezed lemon juice
- 1 tablespoon raw honey or maple syrup
- 1 teaspoon apple cider vinegar
- ¼ teaspoon salt
- 1 tablespoon chopped fresh mint leaves

Directions:

1. Put the chunks of peach in a medium bowl. Add the salt, onions, cherries, lemon juice, honey, and vinegar or cider to the mixture.
2. Before serving, let the mixture sit for 30 minutes. Add the mint when you're ready to serve.

Nutritional Info: Calories: 42 Fat: 0g Protein: 1g Carbs: 10g

Tofu-Basil Sauce

Preparation Time: 10 minutes
Cooking time: 0 minutes
Servings: 2 cups

Ingredients:

- 1 (12-ounce / 340-g) package silken tofu
- ½ cup chopped fresh basil
- 2 garlic cloves, lightly crushed
- ½ cup almond butter
- 1 tablespoon fresh lemon juice
- 1 teaspoon salt
- ¼ teaspoon freshly ground black pepper

Directions:

1. Combine the tofu, basil, garlic, almond butter, lemon juice, salt, and pepper in a blender or food processor. until the process is

smooth. Thin with a little water if it's too thick.
Nutritional Info: Calories: 120 Fat: 10g Protein: 6g Carbs: 5g

Creamy Sesame Dressing

Preparation Time: 5 minutes
Cooking time: 0 minutes
Servings: ¾ cup
Ingredients:

- ½ cup canned full-fat coconut milk
- 2 tablespoons tahini
- 2 tablespoons freshly squeezed lime juice
- 1 teaspoon bottled minced garlic
- 1 teaspoon minced fresh chives
- Pinch sea salt

Directions:
1. Coconut milk, tahini, lime juice, garlic, and chives should all be thoroughly combined in a small bowl. This can also be made in a blender.
2. After seasoning with sea salt, place the dressing in a container with a lid.
Nutritional Info: Calories: 40 Fat: 4g Protein: 1g Carbs: 2g

Almond-Hazelnut Milk

Preparation Time: 15 minutes
Cooking time: 0 minutes
Servings: 4 cups

Ingredients:

- ½ cup-soaked raw hazelnuts, drained
- ½ cup-soaked raw almonds, drained
- 4 cups filtered water
- 1 teaspoon raw honey (optional)
- ¼ teaspoon vanilla extract (optional)

Directions:

1. Place the almonds and hazelnuts in a colander and thoroughly rinse them. Add the water after transferring the mixture to a blender. 30 seconds of blending at high speed2

2 . Carefully pour the nut mixture into a large bowl that has been covered with a nut milk bag or another mesh-like material.

3. Squeezing the pulp to extract as much liquid as you can, pick up the top of the bag and pour the liquid into the bowl.

4. Pour the nut milk into a sealable bottle using a funnel. Add vanilla and honey, if using. Shake the bottle vigorously after sealing it.

Nutritional Info: Calories: 85 Fat: 5g Protein: 2g Carbs: 10g

CONCLUTION

While the majority of patients with acute pancreatitis will completely recover, around 25% of those who are diagnosed may have repeated episodes, making the illness chronic. Your chance of developing pancreatic cancer, diabetes, liver failure, and certain other potentially fatal illnesses rises if you have chronic pancreatitis. A pancreatitis diet must be followed not only for healing but also to prevent the condition from advancing to the chronic stage. Some people, such as those with a history of substance abuse, usage of specific prescription drugs, unhealthy eating habits, and genetics, are more prone to developing pancreatitis. Yoga, meditation, and light exercise may help reduce the symptoms, and quitting drinking and smoking is crucial for recovery. Adopting a healthy diet that prioritizes fresh fruits and vegetables, whole grains, and lean proteins is the first step, regardless of whether you have just received a diagnosis of acute or chronic pancreatitis. The book contains information about the pancreas' diet. The Pancreatic Diet Recipe is a healthy eating lifestyle manual for everyone, not a diet book or a diabetic cookbook. In this book, we explain how eating the right foods can protect your pancreas and promote health, whereas eating the wrong foods abuses your pancreas. By adhering to the guidelines given above, you will be able to make food selections that support your pancreas' healthy operation and enable you to lose weight rapidly. This book has a ton of recipes, meal plans, and instructions. It is the best course of treatment for diet-based pancreatitis.

Printed in Great Britain
by Amazon